*Your Mind
Is Your Teacher*

Your Mind Is Your Teacher

Self-Awakening through
Contemplative Meditation

KHENPO GAWANG

Shambhala
Boston & London
2013

Shambhala Publications, Inc.
Horticultural Hall
300 Massachusetts Avenue
Boston, Massachusetts 02115
www.shambhala.com

Translations of verse extracts are by Khenpo Gawang Rinpoche and Gerry Wiener, unless otherwise noted.

English translation of "The Wheel of Analytical Meditation" by Jamgon Mipham Rinpoche (pages 207–216) copyright © 2013 by Khenpo Gawang Rinpoche and Gerry Wiener.

English translation of "The Sutra of the Heart of Transcendent Knowledge" by the Nālandā Translation Committee under the direction of Chögyam Trungpa Rinpoche (pages 163–165), copyright © 1975, 1980 Diana J. Mukpo and the Nālandā Translation Committee. Reprinted by special arrangement.

9 8 7 6 5 4 3 2 1
First Edition

Printed in the United States of America

⊛This edition is printed on acid-free paper that meets the American National Standards Institute z39.48 Standard.
♻This book is printed on 30% postconsumer recycled paper. For more information please visit www.shambhala.com.

Distributed in the United States by Random House, Inc., and in Canada by Random House of Canada Ltd

Designed by Daniel Urban-Brown

LIBRARY OF CONGRESS CATALOGING-IN-PUBLICATION DATA

Nag-dban, Mkhan-po.
Your Mind Is Your Teacher: Self-Awakening through Contemplative Meditation / Khenpo Gawang.—First edition.
pages cm
Includes translation from Tibetan and Sanskrit.
ISBN 978-1-59030-997-1 (pbk. : alk. paper)
1. Meditation—Buddhism. 2. Nag-dban, Mkhan-po. I. Mi-pham-rgya-mtsho, 'Jam-mgon 'Ju, 1846–1912. Dpyad sgom 'khor lo ma. English. II. Tripitaka. Sutrapitaka. Prajñaparamita. Hrdaya. English. III. Title.
BQ5612.N33 2013
294.3'4435—dc23
2012044708

Contents

About This Book

This handbook is designed to lay out the steps to becoming an expert on our true selves through the practice of Contemplative Meditation. Sometimes called analytical meditation, Contemplative Meditation is a sitting practice in which, instead of trying to quiet our thoughts, we apply the thinking capacity of our naturally inquisitive mind. That's why this book is called *Your Mind Is Your Teacher*.

From the Buddhist point of view, the source of our troubles is that we have seriously misunderstood our body and our mind. It is the job of Contemplative Meditation to correct these misperceptions. When you begin to know the true nature of your body and mind, you will feel better about yourself and your life. I know this from my own experience and the experience of many others.

There can be any number of subjects to think about using this method of Contemplative Meditation. In this book we will analyze and contemplate the "four marks of existence," so named because they encompass the totality of existence. They are also known as the Four Seals of the Dharma because they are the hallmarks of the Buddhist path. In brief, the Four Seals are the teachings of multiplicity, impermanence, suffering, and emptiness.

When you understand the first three clearly, then you will automatically know what "emptiness" means: the fact that the ego to which we cling for our sense of identity and well-being is an illusion, and that in reality all things are devoid of any permanent, separate "self." This fourth seal, emptiness, requires an additional level of analysis, which is explored through a commentary on the classic Heart Sutra, a very powerful short text inspired by the Buddha, which is provided here in English translation.

Why would realizing that everything is "empty" of self be the key to our happiness and peace? This idea often puzzles Westerners, since emptiness doesn't sound like much fun or even interesting. But emptiness is not nothingness; it is the complete openness without obstruction that allows everything to occur. That is why it is said that emptiness and appearance are inseparable. We will experience this more and more, over time, as we look deeply into existence with our wisdom mind.

A few words about the traditional sources of this teaching: Since my wish is to be helpful in a practical way to people living in Western cultures of the twenty-first century, even those whose knowledge of Buddhism is at a beginner's level, I have not written a book of philosophical arguments and scholarly citations. However, the content of the book derives from specific texts, as well as several decades as a monastic practitioner and nine years of study at the Buddhist University of Namdroling Monastery in South India, directed by His Holiness Penor Rinpoche, late head of the Palyul lineage of the Nyingma school of Tibetan Buddhism. The Nyingma is the oldest school of Tibetan Buddhism, built on the earliest transmission of the Dharma to Tibet, brought directly from India during the seventh through eleventh centuries.

Tibetan Buddhism belongs to the Mahayana tradition, which emphasizes the ideal of the bodhisattva ("enlightenment being"), one who strives for enlightenment in order to benefit all sentient beings. The two main teachings of the Mahayana are bodhichitta (the "awakened heart" of compassion) and the wisdom of emptiness (*shunyata*), both of which will be of central importance to our discussion.

Different schools of Buddhism describe the seals of the Dharma in slightly different ways and with different wording. The approach here is based on a concise verse text, *The Wheel of Analytical Meditation* (*Chegom Khorloma; dpyad sgom 'khor lo ma*), composed by Jamgon Mipham Rinpoche (1846–1912). An English translation is provided in part five of this book for those who wish to study it.

Jamgon Mipham Rinpoche, my favorite writer and the focus of my university studies, is referred to as Mipham the Great and has been called the most remarkable Tibetan master of the modern era. He was a brilliant scholar of the Nyingma lineage who produced a body of writings that fill more than thirty volumes of his collected works in Tibetan. Because of his accomplishments, he is regarded as a personification of Manjushri, the Bodhisattva of Wisdom.

To present Jamgon Mipham Rinpoche's teaching in an accessible way, I have woven personal experiences into the book, starting with myself as a young boy determined to become a Buddhist monk. I share the parts of my study and practice path that I think will be helpful for Western students in discovering a meaningful and happy life through knowing our precious fundamental nature. I include examples from modern life, since traditional Tibetan examples are likely to be unfamiliar. I try to avoid using too many foreign words, which in my tradition are not only in Tibetan but also in Sanskrit, the ancient language of India in which many classic texts are written. However, it is not always easy to find an exact English equivalent for some of these terms. In some cases it is just as easy to learn the foreign word, and since you will also encounter these foreign terms in other books on Buddhism, it will be helpful to recognize them. A concise glossary provides reminders of the special terms that have been introduced in the chapters.

I urge you to try Contemplative Meditation. In addition to the instructions in this book, you will find support and a community of practitioners on our interactive website, www.YourMindIsYour-Teacher.org, as described at the back of the book (see "About Pema Karpo Meditation Center"). Once you step onto this path, you will begin to look at everything differently, and your habit patterns will naturally dissolve or change for the better. The way of analysis helps us to understand not only ourselves but the true nature of our world.

My heart's wish is that this teaching on the contemplation of the Four Seals may take root in your life and bring about the changes I know are possible to bring you a happy, peaceful life.

Introduction

From Tibet to Tennessee

A Boyhood Dream

I was a curly-haired little boy running around the village with my younger brother pretending we were driving trucks. We had never seen a truck but we had heard about them from the adults who had left the villages to sell yaks. In the same way I had heard about Buddhism because I was born into a Buddhist family, but I had no personal experience with the practices and teachings.

When I was ten years old, I remember monks from the closest monastery being invited to come to remove obstacles for the village through meditation and chanting. There were very few monks and nuns openly practicing at this time in the Tibetan regions, and the monasteries were just being rebuilt after their destruction. These were the first monks to come to the village. I was old enough to take refuge—the first vow of becoming a Buddhist—with them. I remember the monks telling me to regularly recite OM MANI PADME HUM—the mantra that evokes compassion for all sentient beings. They also told me to be careful to not kill bugs and other small creatures.

Later an old lama came to the village to give a long-life empowerment ritual. After he left, a group of us children would pretend we were holding empowerments. We made up prayers that we would chant loudly and pretend we were playing the traditional horns and cymbals. We made shrines from rocks and sticks, and our offerings were dust on flat rocks. It was great fun.

It was after the visits of the monks and the old lama that I began to tell my parents I wanted to become a monk. This frightened them, as they had experienced the wrath of the Communist Chinese soldiers in the 1950s and '60s. At first they tried to dissuade me because of the possible danger, but I was persistent. Finally they gave their permission, and I became a monk.

My time of driving imaginary trucks and pretending empowerments with my friends and brother alternated with learning to read and write Tibetan and to chant daily prayers. As I grew older, I spent more and more time at the Gompa Tsang monastery, close to my village area. There I learned the ritual practices and chanting. I participated fully in empowerments and learned to play the actual instruments and to make the beautiful offerings called tormas, ritual cakes molded from butter and flour.

On a visit home, a friend of my father's, named Gundra, came to stay for a few days. He told us about a wonderful old yogi, Khenpo Karma Tsepten, who had lived for many years at a monastery called Tachog Gonpa, very high in the mountains. He had started living there alone, but later people found him and came to study with him as his students. Gundra said that this teacher gave the high teachings known as Dzogchen every year, and if you received them you would be enlightened very, very quickly. I decided I wanted to meet him and receive these teachings that would lead to rapid enlightenment. I told my father I wanted to go to this monastery and meet this great teacher.

Up until then I had been learning to read and write, chant, and do liturgical activities, but I had not begun to study the important Buddhist texts and commentaries of the great masters. Many times I had heard people say an amazing thing about the Dzogchen "pointing-out instructions," in which a master directly reveals the "nature of mind" to the student. It was said that a student could begin the teaching session as an ordinary person seated on the ground and, after receiving and understanding the teachings, arise as an enlightened being. I really wanted this.

After the visit of my father's old friend, I was always thinking about Khenpo Karma Tsepten and longing to go to this monastery to receive these precious teachings. At first my mother and father agreed, thinking it was a good idea. It took me a few years to prepare to make the trip.

Learning from a Great Yogi

When I was about seventeen years old I heard that some local yak herders were going to a place to purchase barley that was just a four-day walk from Khenpo Karma Tsepten's monastery. I and three of my monastic friends made a plan to accompany them and then walk on to this monastery.

Traveling with the yak herders for the first part of the journey would make things much easier because it would be safe and the yaks could carry our luggage. We decided to leave early in the day. That morning my father was very concerned that I was actually going to make this long trip. After a little while passed and we had talked about it, he accepted it. My parents packed clothing, barley flour, cheese, butter, and meat for the trip and sent me off with their best wishes.

After four days we arrived at the yak herders' destination, where we stayed with a lovely host family who were in the midst of preparing a field for planting. We spent the day helping break up the ground to repay their kindness. In the evening we ground the barley we were taking with us to eat at the monastery. The final leg of the trip began auspiciously when our hosts found us a thirty-minute truck ride in the direction of the monastery. It still took four days of steady walking from early morning until night to reach the monastery. It was atop the highest mountain in the area, overlooking all the other snow-covered peaks.

We went immediately to Khenpo Karma Tsepten's place and waited outside the fence. We could hear him inside coughing. His attendant invited us in to meet him at his retreat cabin, which was half cave, half house. It had a porch where he used to sit and teach the students seated in the front yard.

When I first saw him he was sitting on the porch on an old yak skin rug, wearing simple robes, with shoulder-length white hair, a long white beard, and very thick glasses over which he wore a pair of sunglasses to help with reading. He was very, very old. We offered prostrations, and then I introduced our group, giving our history. I explained that we had traveled a long distance to his place to receive Dzogchen teachings and requested that he accept us as his students. Khenpo Karma Tsepten did accept all four of us.

At the time we arrived, he was teaching a famous text by Shantideva, a great master and scholar from eighth-century India. This text, the *Bodhicharyavatara* (The Way of the Bodhisattva), is about the six transcendental virtues, called *paramitas,* which are practiced by a bodhisattva. He was teaching the chapter on patience. He recommended that we stay and receive this teaching first, because afterward he was going to offer Dzogchen teachings from the *Yeshe Lama,* an important text by the eighteenth-century master Jigme Lingpa.

Every day he would teach in the morning for one or two hours. He would sit on the porch of his retreat hut, and we would sit on our shoes in the yard. It would snow almost every night, and sometimes it would be snowing while Khenpo Karma Tsepten was teaching. When it snowed, we would pull our monk's shawls up over our heads and the text to protect it from the blowing snowflakes.

My friends and I had no experience with studying a text. The Khenpo would read a little and then give a commentary, but we didn't know this and spent a lot of time hunting for where he was in the text. He was a thorough teacher who explained each part very slowly and very carefully, with much detail. Senior students would gather a group of us during the afternoons and evenings and go over what he had taught in the morning. We would have long discussions. Slowly we began to be able to follow what the Khenpo was teaching.

When Shantideva's text was finished, he did begin the Dzogchen teachings. Khenpo Tsepten would give a short teaching, as was his style, every morning. Then we would do the practices in the afternoon and evening. We trained like this for many months, receiving teachings and then doing the attendant practices. The Khenpo would send us out to meditate individually in isolated spots on the mountaintop. The mountaintop had great views conducive to this type of meditation, especially when the sun was rising and setting.

I quickly discovered I was not the type of person who sat down to receive the beginning empowerment and then stood up enlightened. However, to this day I am very grateful that at an early age I was able to receive these profound teachings from a realized Dzogchen master.

Pilgrimage and Studies

When I was nineteen, I felt I was ready to begin a serious and deep study of the central texts and commentaries of Tibetan Buddhism. This would require me to go to a Buddhist college called a *shedra*. To prepare for the upcoming nine years of intensive study, I first went on a pilgrimage to the main places of importance in the life of Shakyamuni Buddha. I visited his birthplace, Lumbini, in Nepal and then Kushingara, in India, where the Buddha passed away; Vulture Peak Mountain, where he taught the *Prajnaparamita Sutra;* and the site of Nalanda University in the Indian state of Bihar.

After visiting Nalanda I arrived in Bodhgaya, the place of the Buddha's enlightenment, where the Nyingma Monlam Chenmo, a great gathering of prayers for world peace, was taking place, and so I stayed for the ten days of practice. In Bodhgaya, to my great good fortune, I met His Holiness Penor Rinpoche and requested his permission to come to his monastery, Namdroling, in South India and study at his Buddhist college, Namdroling Shedra.

He said yes and to please talk to the finance person to ask for a train ticket to Namdroling Monastery. We talked to the person in charge and he said okay, but when I went to the train station there wasn't an individual ticket waiting for me. The monks in charge told me to get on with the other thousands of monks going back to Namdroling and there would be no problem finding a place to stay on the train.

Looking at the extremely crowded train and knowing that I would be on it not for hours but for days, I decided to wait and go to Sarnath, the place where the Buddha first taught the Four Noble Truths. From there I went to Dharamsala to meet His Holiness the fourteenth Dalai Lama. This had been a heart's wish since I was very young.

After meeting His Holiness the Dalai Lama, I took a less crowded train to South India. At the Namdroling Shedra I began nine years of intensive study and practice with the same text I studied on the mountaintop with Khenpo Karma Tsepten—the *Bodhicharyavatara* by Shantideva. This beautiful and passionate text begins in the same way I wish to begin this book—with the reminder that we are very lucky and already blessed just to have been born into a human form with the precious opportunity to receive and practice the Dharma:

> These free and well-favored conditions are extremely hard
>   to find.
> Having obtained this human body and the opportunity to
>   help all sentient beings,
> If you fail to practice the Dharma that accomplishes benefit,
> How will you ever get this excellent chance again in future
>   lives?
>   —SHANTIDEVA, *The Way of the Bodhisattva,* translated by
>   the Padmakara Translation Group

Starting a New Life

The nine years I spent studying and living at Namdroling Monastery flew by. The last year I was there, my friend Sakyong Mipham Rinpoche called and invited me to come to America. I had never considered going to the West, and I didn't speak English. My root teacher, His Holiness Penor Rinpoche, called me to his residence and told me he wanted me to go. For four years I traveled with Sakyong Mipham Rinpoche, mainly within Shambhala International. This was helpful to me, as I naturally began to learn about Western culture and Buddhist students.

I still didn't learn much English because I was always planning to go back to Namdroling. I assumed I was going to teach in Tibetan at the Buddhist college there and that my whole life would be immersed in the monastic Tibetan Buddhist world. I had already taught for three years and found I loved it.

In my fourth year, I began to reconsider my assumptions. There were many good teachers at Namdroling and more were being trained. If, instead of returning there, I lived in America, I could be helpful in bringing Buddhism to the West. This change in my view then led to the next question: where should I go? I was invited to visit Memphis, Tennessee, to see if it felt like an auspicious place for me. Meeting sincere students there, I felt it was a good place to establish my Dharma center, Pema Karpo. I enrolled in English classes at a local university and began to hold meditation sessions.

At first, giving just a three-minute talk in English was very difficult. It seemed to take forever to get the words out, but at least we could all meditate together in silence. To this day I continue to meditate along with the students at our twice-weekly sessions because I feel it is important for teacher and students to practice together. Today, I can speak for an hour or more in English and the time flies by swiftly.

Finally I had the great opportunity to take the U.S. citizenship exam. I studied very hard to pass the test and learned a lot of

American history and law. The principles this country was founded upon are amazing. Because of our First Amendment rights—including freedom of religion and freedom of assembly—people of all faiths, or no religious faith, can come and go freely at Pema Karpo, united in our common wish to practice the Dharma. "Life, liberty, and the pursuit of happiness" could be another way of expressing basic Dharma. We have our human life, we have the liberty to discover our true nature, and we can and should pursue happiness by understanding the true causes of happiness. These are the rights of all sentient beings.

I am glad I decided to stay in the United States. I passed the citizenship test and in July 2011 became a citizen. My path of being helpful to others and my own Dharma practice have grown stronger from this unexpected change in my life. Recently a new student asked me, "Are you happy?" and I could honestly reply, "Yes, I am happy!"

Part One

Contemplative Meditation

1

Happiness Is in Your Hands

The more we know ourselves, the happier we will be.

This is essentially a book about happiness. Everyone wants happiness, but for some reason we can't seem to achieve the happiness we long for or to hold on to it for very long. Why not?

If we look closely and honestly at ourselves, analyzing our everyday experience, we are likely to find that we are caught up in repetitive patterns of negative thinking, disturbing emotions, and habitual speech and behaviors that keep us from finding satisfaction and fulfillment. Our many troubles have their basis in misperception, misunderstanding, and a lack of knowledge. We don't know how to get out of the tangle of troubles we find ourselves caught in.

Buddhism has been studying the nature of this problem over the course of more than twenty-five centuries, guided by the teachings of Shakyamuni Buddha, which are known as the Buddha Dharma. The Dharma is a set of universal teachings, meant for everyone, not just Buddhists, monks and nuns, or philosophers. And even though they originated in ancient times, these teachings are not difficult to practice in the modern world, even for those without special training. To learn how to eliminate the obstacles to happiness, you don't have to spend years studying difficult books, learning foreign languages, or spending long periods in solitude. As long as you apply effort on a regular basis, you can use your ordinary daily life and human faculties as the tools for transforming your troubles into peace and happiness.

Without going to any special place or adopting unusual customs, you already have everything you need for spiritual practice. Your sacred place of retreat is your body. Your daily life is your practice center. Your emotions, thoughts, and experiences are your instructors. And even if you don't realize it at the moment, you possess a mind that is fundamentally clear and peaceful. This authentic wisdom-mind is your ultimate teacher.

What exactly is the happiness that we all want? I think we would all welcome having more satisfaction in our lives and feeling more connected to other people, animals, and the environment. A radical idea to consider is that we could be satisfied simply by having sufficient money to pay the bills, enough food and clean water, comfortable clothing, and shelter from the elements. Additionally, if we are healthy, secure, and not being looked for by the police, then these would be causes for rejoicing. Maybe what our society or culture tells us is indispensable—things such as gourmet foods and luxury clothing, exciting entertainments, a good-looking boyfriend or girlfriend, and success that brings praise, fame, and wealth—is not truly the essence of a joyful life.

Let me propose something else that may be even more radical: that we are already perfect in being exactly who we are. Each of us is uniquely who we are, and this is a good thing. To try to be like someone else or different from our own nature is a direct path to unhappiness.

I don't mean that it's unnecessary to make any changes at all. For example, it is a good idea to stop doing things that cause harm to ourselves and others, and to strengthen qualities that bring happiness to ourselves and others. In particular, if we could change our motivation so that what we seek most is the upliftment of oth-

Much more important than money, possessions, or status is our inner or mental state of being. Members of a poor family will be happy if there is affection, kindness, and trust between them. Their rich neighbors may live in luxury, but if suspicion or resentment besets their minds, they will have no genuine happiness. This is a matter of common sense. So ultimately the mental level is key.

—His Holiness the Dalai Lama, *Beyond Religion*

---

er beings, that would be the wisest kind of change. Those kinds of changes are good. But in addition, I am suggesting that we could accept, appreciate, and perhaps, with time, come to love the body and mind we were born with. According to the teachings of the Buddha, being human is the best possible birth in the world, and this is an important cause for happiness that is usually overlooked in our world. Later on, we will see in greater detail what the Buddha meant by the teaching of "precious human birth."

Still, the million-dollar question is *how* to bring the mind to a state of happiness, contentment, and peace. Self-knowledge is the answer—becoming aware of what we are, physically and mentally. Contemplative Meditation is the answer.

I find it both interesting and sad that often we do not know the person who is the closest to us—our own self. Hiding from ourselves causes much more trouble than anything we will discover by looking closely and clearly. The core Buddhist teachings are about revealing our true self; therefore self-knowledge is the best knowledge to acquire. When we speak of self-knowledge, we are referring to our true nature, not to the ego-self that we hang on to, worry so much about, and are always protecting. That self cannot be found. This is what Shakyamuni Buddha discovered when he looked deeply into the reality of our world. We cling to what does not exist in ways that only give us trouble and make our lives harder. So if you read this book with the intention of knowing yourself, and then put the teachings into action, it will definitely lead to changes that will bring about more happiness and less suffering.

"Suffering" is a word one often sees in Buddhist teachings, but "dissatisfaction" may be closer to what is meant as a chronic condition. In many parts of the world, people's sufferings are physical—a desperate search for enough food, water, shelter, medical care, and safety. In the West we have a decent standard of living and relative safety, but we have a lot of mental suffering, with isolation, stress, addiction, dissatisfaction, and epidemic levels of low self-worth. Everyone has to pass through the problems and frustrations of childhood and adolescence. If we live a full life, we will experience sickness, aging, a period when the body breaks down, the loss of friends and family, and finally our own death.

The list of worries, frustrations, disappointments, and losses is unique to each person, but all who are alive have experienced them. Yet the Buddha very clearly identified that the reason for our suffering is not external difficulties, but the fact that we don't know our own nature ("ignorance"). If we can gain even a small understanding of the truth of this teaching, then we will be taking a wrecking ball to the foundation of the troubling mental patterns that keep us from enjoying our natural state of peace.

Through the practice of contemplation, we gradually transform our view—the reality that we take to be the truth—and this new outlook will transform our experience of everyday life. Let me give a simple example of how an experienced contemplator might flip a troubling situation in ordinary life. Take something we all know, a birthday party. So there you are, ripping the paper off a present, only to discover something totally inappropriate or something that you really don't want. Maybe your cousin grabbed something at the last moment without thinking, or maybe a friend is giving you a "gift" meant to make you feel bad.

You have two main choices. You can hold tight to any feelings of anger, dislike, depression, or unhappiness that arise, and your body and your mind will feel stressed and troubled. Or you can accept the unwelcome gift that you have unwrapped, just seeing it in a neutral way and move on.

It is the same gift, but the way of thinking about it makes a big difference in the quality of life. If the reaction is kept neutral, then even a present given with a bad attitude and meant to harm cannot ruin the birthday party. What we are working for here is being able to accept the life we have, and what we do not have, in a more balanced and less emotionally painful way.

When I first moved to the United States, my next-door neighbor was an elderly woman who had become interested in Buddhism after seeing His Holiness the Dalai Lama on TV. She asked me if I had any of his books she could read. Loaning her books led to a friendship, and she confided to me that she had a daughter she had not seen for twenty-five years. As she told the story of the estrangement, I could see that the events that caused it were as real to her now as they had been all those years ago. She was still filled with anger, resentment, and bitterness about the way her daughter had behaved toward her as a teenager.

Even though my English was not so good then, I got across that holding on to these negative emotions only harmed her. She had been keeping them alive inside herself about a situation that had not existed for a quarter century. Yet again and again in her mind she continued to fight with a teenage daughter who in reality was now forty years old. To put the problem in Dharma terms, my neighbor had taken as permanent what in reality is impermanent.

I tell this story to show one of the main reasons that we need to engage in Contemplative Meditation. All of us have such conceptual beliefs and habitual behaviors operating in our lives, behind the scenes, but we may have never stopped to examine them closely. What are some of the main patterns that most of us will see in ourselves? We will see resistance to change; we will see how we take things personally; and we will notice that we cling to an image of ourselves as an invariable, unified "I." We have never analyzed these habits to see whether they are based on the truth or even make sense at all. If we did, we would realize that many of our interpretations and assumptions are based on misconceptions. These misconceptions are often the underlying cause of anxious thoughts and painful emotional states. One of the most common misconceptions is this habit of assuming in our mind that things, people, and experiences are permanent, when in fact they change constantly or are even no longer in existence. It is essential that we observe and really see these patterns in action.

We cannot change these patterns by wishing they would go away. We have to work hard, using our power of investigation again and again. Using Contemplative Meditation as a method of gentle self-analysis, we can begin to uncover the root causes of our troublesome habits. We begin by noticing our mental and emotional patterns without even trying to do anything about them. We just want to look at these patterns very clearly, with a kind and loving attitude toward ourselves. Then, based on clear reasoning, we will be able to see the fallacies in our thought patterns and start to change them. Not only that, but they will even break down naturally and dissolve by themselves, because they are not in accord with the way things are.

Often when an uncomfortable or painful situation occurs, there is an automatic blaming of someone or something outside of ourselves. The Buddhist method, when such a situation occurs, is to begin by looking, without blame, internally at our mind. Very often what we find is that we ourselves placed the burr that is making us buck under our saddle. As contemplative meditators we want to become more like lions than dogs, as in the following analogy:

Lord Buddha taught that there are two ways to meditate—like a dog and like a lion. If you throw a stick at a dog, he will chase after the stick; but if you throw a stick at a lion, the lion will chase after you. You can throw as many sticks as you like at a dog, but at a lion only one. When you are completely barraged with thoughts, chasing after each one in turn with its antidote is an endless task. That is like the dog. It is better, like the lion, to look for the source of those thoughts, void awareness, on whose surface thoughts move like ripples on the surface of a lake, but whose depth is the unchanging state of utter simplicity.

—DILGO KHYENTSE RINPOCHE, *The Heart Treasure of the Enlightened Ones*

What is "void awareness"? The Dharma teaches that the fundamental nature of our mind is emptiness, which is unchangeable. Thus, paradoxically, there is nothing to change. Our nature is perfect clarity, peacefulness, and happiness. But because we don't understand these qualities, it appears that we have to change. Actually, the only thing we can and must change are the habitual patterns that cover up our original nature. In the process of self-awakening, most of what will occur is a change of perception—a new view of reality. This change of view comes about thanks to the wisdom arising from the practice of Contemplative Meditation and the dissolving of mistaken concepts and negative emotions.

The big secret to happiness is that once we are free from the misperceptions and emotional obscurations that cause problems, we find that the pure self we were born with is naturally happy. We won't need to add anything to create happiness.

The nature of our mind is enlightenment, but right now this is covered by mistaken concepts and negative emotions. When these are completely dissolved, enlightenment, which is ultimate happiness, naturally occurs.

Both temporary and ultimate happiness are the result of our actions, so we have to create the causes for this happiness through our body, speech, and most important, our mind. The goal of becoming more happy and peaceful in everyday life and the goal of enlightenment are closely connected. It is another paradox that in order to be deeply happy ourselves, we must care about the happiness of others.

The best way to achieve temporary and ultimate happiness is to develop a bigger view. The first step is motivation or bodhichitta, which is the heartfelt wish to help all sentient beings become enlightened and so attain ultimate happiness. Awakening and strengthening bodhichitta is the path of the bodhisattvas, who are great beings dedicated to benefiting others.

Happiness Checklist

√ Appreciate that being human is the best possible birth in the world.
√ Be content with good things that you have.
√ Choose to have a neutral attitude about unpleasant events.
√ Do meritorious actions to lay the foundation for a happier life.
√ Do no harmful actions.
√ Change your motivation to seeking the upliftment and happiness of others.
√ Free yourself from misperceptions, negative habit patterns, and disturbing emotions.
√ Discover that the pure self you were born with is naturally happy.

2

The Thinker's Guide to Enlightenment

Thinking and conceptual mind are not the problem; the problem is the way we get hooked by our thoughts and emotions.

Many times I hear students say, "I don't want to think—I just want to sit." They fear that any analytical process is too "mental" and will only lead to more of the conceptual, discursive thinking that already overburdens the Western approach to life. For example, one time, when I led a program on Contemplative Meditation, one of the participants asked me for a private interview after my opening talk. She told me, "I do not want more concepts. I just want to rest my mind." I replied, "I do not want more concepts either, but we all already have a lot of concepts in our minds. We need to put them to use in a good way that is helpful." At the end of the program I saw this participant again, and now, after practicing contemplation, she told me that her view had changed. She saw for herself that it was not about adding more mental concepts.

I have another student who describes her mind as a jackhammer. Obviously none of us wants lots of thoughts and emotions noisily busting up our peace, but if that is what we have, we can work with it. We can use our conceptual mind in a way that will actually lead to a more peaceful and contented mind. To get this

Look at your mind with mind.
Since it cannot be identified, it is like space.
Not seeing anything whatsoever, it is crystal clarity.
Its essential nature abides in emptiness.

From within the nature of unobstructed emptiness
Appearances are unceasing, vivid, and sharp.
They are without partiality, all-pervasive and
  unconditioned.
This luminous nature—what a great wonder.

—JAMGON MIPHAM RINPOCHE, *The Meditation and Recitation of the Six-Syllable Avalokiteshvara,* translated by Khenpo Gawang Rinpoche and Gerry Wiener

---

mind, we initially have to do a lot of observation and thinking about it. It is interesting, and a little humorous, to realize that thinking could be the way to bring an end to a lot of unnecessary thinking. I would offer for consideration that thinking and having a conceptual mind are not the problem, but how we get hooked and hoodwinked by our thoughts and emotions.

Two Types of Meditation: Resting and Insight

The different Buddhist lineages emphasize different kinds of meditation, but they can all be classified as one of two general categories: resting meditation (*shamatha* in Sanskrit and *shi-ne* in Tibetan) and insight meditation (Skt. *vipashyana;* Tib. *lhakthong*). Contemplative Meditation practice falls into the second category, vipashyana.

Resting meditation aims to still the mind—to let go of thoughts or allow thoughts to settle down—in order to experience peace or release stress. The objective is to cultivate a mind that is not disturbed by mental wandering. Vipashyana makes it possible to gain insight into the true nature of reality. It's not insight in the ordinary usage of the word, but in the sense of becoming familiar with the way things really are. The Tibetan term for vipashyana, *lhakthong*, literally means "special seeing."

We are using the term "Contemplative Meditation" for this practice of analytical meditation so that the idea of "analysis" won't scare people off. This is not an intellectual exercise for philosophers. It is more like using our normal ability to think clearly, with our natural sense of inquisitiveness, about any topic that is meaningful to us. The only difference is that we apply this ability in a formal sitting practice.

It's significant that the Tibetan word for meditation, *gom,* means "to become familiar with." In practicing Contemplative Meditation, first we analyze our chosen subject matter until we are completely familiar with it. Once we have become familiar with the subject, we can rest in the understanding without thinking analytically. Thus, both contemplative and resting meditation slow down the discursive mind.

Without meditation—both contemplative and resting—our mind is filled with many concepts, thoughts, and emotional states, like rainy-day driving in a busy city during rush hour. Mentally we have the honking horns, taxis, buses, and all the other drivers hunched over their wheels trying to get somewhere. With meditation, our mind can slow down and our thoughts lessen. Now it is like driving with the top down on a beautiful day in the countryside. We have the mental equivalent of flowers, trees, and beautiful views, with a straight road and few cars.

So how do we arrive at this state of mind that, like a drive in the country, leads to relaxation, contentment, and happiness? Contemplative Meditation uses our intelligence and our honed ability to think, in order to help gradually dissolve our unhelpful and troublesome habit patterns, along with confused thoughts and emotional states, and experience our calm, relaxed, and clear wisdom mind.

When I first came to the West, I saw that many Buddhist

practitioners were interested in resting meditation, but they were neglecting the analytical practices. As I got to know Western students better, I saw that they had sharp, well-trained minds, formed through their educational system, which could understand the Contemplative Meditation practices I had been taught.

Without an understanding of self, and particularly mind, I think it is very difficult to tame our mind. I am not criticizing resting meditation, but if we do not have a clear understanding of mind, then the pitfall of dullness and lethargy can impede our progress, sending us in the wrong direction. From a Dharma point of view, knowing ourselves is the cause of wisdom and the way to eliminate confusion. So many of the views we hold about ourselves and our world are habitual mental patterns. We want to observe these habit patterns first and then begin to change the confused and troublesome patterns into wise and helpful patterns.

We need a clear mind-training map to keep us from missing the correct path. If we want to go to New York, we need to know the roads and directions. Just jumping in the car and starting to drive may get us there, but most likely we will end up in another place or take much longer than is necessary.

I have seen this happen with students who tell me of doing years of meditation without seeing any changes. They may blame themselves, meditation, or the Dharma, yet most often the problem is not knowing or applying the correct techniques or methods. Meditation is both easy and not easy. With the correct techniques and methods, applied with diligence, meditation can become a swift path to clearing confusion and unhelpful habits. Without them, we may wander in fogginess or agitation, never having engaged in true meditation even after years of "sitting."

At Namdroling Monastery we practiced both resting and analytical meditation. The renowned teacher Jamgon Mipham Rinpoche believed that both types of meditation were important, but he thought it was best to begin with analytical meditation, because gaining familiarity with the true nature of reality would

Once you have gained familiarity, you won't find anything
to be difficult.

— SHANTIDEVA, *Bodhicharyavatara*

---

naturally lead to a clearer understanding of resting meditation and
how to engage our mind constructively, with less risk of mistakes
and sidetracks. He added that after we became familiar with the
true nature, it would be unnecessary to continue to investigate
and analyze, and that we could give more and more emphasis to
resting meditation.

Mindfulness and Awareness

Before we begin Contemplative Meditation as a practice, it is
helpful, in the long run, to spend a little time looking at our usual
thoughts and beliefs. For the meditation to be effective, the mind
needs to be able to stay with one subject long enough to become familiar with the topic and develop insight. Most of us have an unruly
mind that jumps everywhere like a monkey playing in the trees.

In a broad sense, we can consider our mind to have three main
parts: thoughts and emotions, mindfulness, and awareness. To help
understand what this means, imagine yourself driving on a busy
freeway at rush hour. Your body is the car. The act of driving is
your *thoughts and emotions*—the forces that "drive" the actions of
your body. Remembering the rules and laws of the road, where
you are, and where you are going is *mindfulness*. Noticing the environment in which you are driving, and how the cars all around
you are moving, is *awareness*. In meditation, you are asking your
awareness, the part of your mind that you use when you notice
all the other drivers around you, to pay attention to your personal
thoughts and emotions.

Mindfulness and awareness are essential to any type of meditation. Without mindfulness and awareness, you cannot contemplate

in a meaningful, clear, and inquisitive fashion. Mindfulness keeps you from forgetting the object of contemplation, and awareness holds the mind to the contemplation, recognizes when attention has shifted to something else, and brings it back. It is helpful if you can recognize these three parts of your mind early on in your practice. If you can identify them, then you can strengthen the mindfulness and awareness and not be discouraged by the discursiveness of thoughts and emotions.

If you have a moment, lay this book down for a few minutes and contemplate your own mind-stream of thoughts and beliefs about yourself. How comfortable are you in your body and mind? Is your mind relaxed, clear, and peaceful? Do you feel connected to your body, the world around you, and the center of your own life? Are you aware of habitual patterns that keep causing you trouble again and again?

Overview of the Practice

A summary of how we practice Contemplative Meditation will help orient you to the series of steps that are explained in the chapters that follow.

The Preliminary Steps

Contemplative Meditation is a sitting practice in which we are seated comfortably on a meditation cushion or a chair, with an upright posture and deep, smooth breathing. We prepare ourselves for the main contemplations by using supportive thoughts and images that motivate us to practice:

Precious human birth (chapter 3). We rouse our mind to make a joyful effort by remembering that our human life is precious and that the practice we are about to do is important.

Visualization (chapter 4). We connect with the omniscient and compassionate Buddha through a simple practice of visualization.

Accumulating merit (chapter 5). Whenever we want to accomplish something, we usually face difficulties and obstacles before we complete the project. Seven steps, called the Seven-Branch Offering, are used to assure that strength and good fortune, or merit, will accumulate within us and help us to succeed.

Awakening bodhichitta (chapter 6). Sometimes called "awakened heart," bodhichitta is the wish to achieve buddhahood in order to benefit others. Bodhichitta is the major mental condition that we need in order to develop a mind with stable and lasting happiness, joy, peace, and mental well-being. We resolve to remove all our confusion and misperceptions so that we can be helpful to as many sentient beings as possible. The seed of the awakened heart is naturally within us. I will be teaching you three methods that have been used over hundreds of years to awaken this wonderful bodhichitta.

The Dedication of Merit. The closing (see pages 50–53) is a practice of generosity in which we give away the merit—all the goodness and benefit that result from our practice—to all sentient beings.

The Objects of Contemplation

The focal point of our Contemplative Meditation—the objects of our investigation—will be four subjects. Everything that the Buddha taught is directly or indirectly related to these four subjects. They are called the Four Seals, since they are the mark or stamp of the Buddha's teachings. Sometimes they are called the "four marks of existence" because they encompass the totality of existence. Each one is summarized simply here, and later I explain them in more detail.

The Four Seals

- *Impermanence* (chapter 7): The nature of life is change and impermanence; yet we take what is impermanent to be permanent.

- *Multiplicity* (chapter 8): Everything that exists is composed of a multiplicity of ever-changing parts; yet we believe that we are singular, a unified whole.
- *Suffering* (chapter 9): We do things that cause suffering, even though we really want peace and happiness.
- *Emptiness* (chapter 10): Our true nature is emptiness, a state of openness and peace, like a clear and cloudless sky, undisturbed by negative thoughts and emotions, and free from mistaken perceptions or concepts of reality.

We are always changing, and there is nothing we can do about this; *impermanence* is just a fact of life. We are composed of a *multiplicity* of different parts, both physical and nonphysical. A singular permanent "I" cannot be found, yet we cling to our idea of "me" and "mine," and this causes *suffering*. However, we have the potential to awaken to the true nature of reality, which is *emptiness*, the ultimate peace and happiness called nirvana.

Impermanence, the first seal, is easy to understand by looking at everyday experiences. Think about that little shock you receive when you meet an old friend you have not seen in a few years and he has changed unexpectedly: he's become heavier or thinner, more or less healthy, divorced or married. In your mind he had stayed exactly the same as he was the last time you saw him; that's why seeing the change gave you a shock. But after spending a little time with your friend, your old view of him naturally dissolves in the face of the new reality, and now you can accept that he has changed in some respects.

Multiplicity is the next hallmark of existence. Everything in our world, including us, is made up of parts. A famous teaching story from India describes a person mistaking a coil of rope for a poisonous snake and then reacting in great fear. This is the predicament most of us find ourselves in. We mistake an ever-changing pile of various things to be a person that we call "me." The minute you turn your flashlight on and see that the "snake" is just a rope, all fear instantly disappears. Similarly, as long as we hold on tight to this misconception of a permanent, unitary "me," we are headed for trouble. When we accept that we are made up of many ever-changing parts, living in an ever-changing world also made up of many parts, our minds are going to relax and our emotional upheavals will lessen.

We have a body made up of trillions of cells, of blood, bones, fat, skin, hair, and other components. Our mind, too, can be divided into countless factors. Think about how many thoughts we have in one hour and how many different emotions arise in one day. Looking carefully in this way, over and over again, we will find it very hard to find a single "me" that lasts for more than a few seconds. Seeing that everything is made up of so many different changing parts helps us let go of our belief that there is any one singular thing to be found on planet Earth.

Analyzing the third seal, suffering, we begin to see that it, too, is not a fixed reality. We investigate the causes of suffering in our many negative or false mind states—our disturbing emotions and misconceptions—and the ego-clinging that results from our identification with an illusory self.

The last hallmark of existence is emptiness, which equates with peace (nirvana). Here the meaning of peace is very different from the absence of war, aggression, or violence. In this context, peace means an absence of disturbing concepts, thoughts, and emotions. We pray that all sentient beings will recognize this inner peace that is their true nature. It is not possible to have true world peace without individuals who completely recognize their true nature. Peace can also mean freedom from the physical and mental factors that condition existence. "Conditioned existence" is another term for samsara, the cyclic realm of being in which all phenomena are dependent on the law of causality and the existence of one thing is dependent on that of others.

Emptiness is also equated with selflessness, meaning the absence of self as a solid, permanent entity. In Contemplative Meditation we ask: Who is this self we are so attached to? Who is suffering? Is it mind or is it body? Mentally, we begin to take our body apart and look at the details of our physical being. Then we do the same thing to our mind, examining all of its many aspects. We are not going to find a self. You can look and look and look—and I encourage you to do it—but after over twenty-five hundred years of looking, no one has ever found a self.

The best description of the last seal, emptiness, is found in the Heart Sutra. Because of its importance in helping us understand emptiness, nirvana, and selflessness, I give special attention to the Heart Sutra by presenting a detailed commentary on it in part five.

Contemplative Meditation will not always rely on all four seals. The first three—impermanence, multiplicity, and suffering—are temporary. They must be understood and accepted completely in the beginning. But a mind that relies only on them cannot be stable if the basis—consisting of these three seals—is unstable.

Contemplative Meditation that is stable is based on a mind familiar with emptiness: the unchanging fundamental nature, as it is—unmade and uncreated. When our mind is familiar with this nature, then we have stability, because there is the union of object and subject. Concepts are transformed into nonconceptual wisdom, which is experiential.

Jamgon Mipham Rinpoche wrote a short Tibetan text in verse called *The Wheel of Analytical Meditation* that teaches this method of contemplating the Four Seals. An English version of it is given in part five. I remember during my studies when a classmate invited me to join a small group preparing to do extracurricular study of this text. It was being offering during tea break by one of the senior teachers, Khenchen Pema Sherab Rinpoche, in his room. There was one verse in particular that struck me with great force:

Consider the merit of someone who, for one thousand deity
    years,
Meets all the needs of the Three Jewels,
Providing them whatever they require.

By comparison, if one examines the suffering,
Impermanence, emptiness, and selflessness of conditioned
  existence,
For just the time it takes to snap one's fingers,
The merit gained is immeasurably more exalted, as said in
  the sutras.

This verse says that even a moment's reflection on the Four Seals is more meritorious than serving the Three Jewels—Buddha, Dharma, and Sangha—for a thousand cosmic years. If you understand impermanence, multiplicity, suffering, and emptiness, you will have understood the entirety of the Buddha's teachings—as if you had studied thousands of sutras in the time it takes to snap your fingers!

The stability, clarity, and nonconceptual wisdom that we are able to awaken in our mind through contemplation will go with us from lifetime to lifetime until we attain enlightenment. In the *Guhyagarbha* it is said:

Because the nature of mind is complete enlightenment,
There is no other enlightenment to search for.
Even if the buddhas were to search,
They would find no other place.

Benefits of Contemplative Meditation

The regular practice of Contemplative Meditation helps us to:

√ Know and understand ourselves, and be more in touch with our true nature
√ Overcome negative emotions and lead happier, more peaceful lives, free from self-created suffering
√ Let go of habitual unwholesome patterns of behavior and thought that cover up our original nature

√ Train our minds for better concentration and clearer perception

√ Experience more peace and mental well-being

√ Increase our sense of self-worth

√ Gain the confidence of knowing that the life we were born with gives us the best possible cause for happiness

---

Part Two

*Preliminary
Steps*

3

Precious Human Birth

We should embrace ourselves as we are, because being human is the best possible birth in the world.

Being human has many freedoms. It doesn't mean that life is perfect and we always get what we want, but if we consider carefully, we realize that as humans who aspire to a spiritual life, we have so many great qualities and potentials.

Having a positive outlook about ourselves becomes easier if we reflect on the less fortunate state of many other beings. Most of us are fortunate not to be living in a war zone where people suffer from injury, torture, and rape, the loss of life and limb, and the destruction of homes and property. However, some of us may have family in the armed forces and we all can see in the media what it is like for those living in painful conditions that we have not had to face. We are not too hungry or thirsty, too cold or hot, or under such severe stress that we can only try to stay alive. Instead, even if we don't have an easy life, we still have the freedom to pursue some of our interests, such as reading a Dharma book.

Sometimes I watch the Military Channel on cable, learning about wars of the past and present. Watching the documentaries or reenactments becomes an opportunity for me to generate compassion for everyone who is affected by the sufferings and upheaval of war. Our history is filled with violence, a result of being born as human beings, with mixed qualities and thus the ability to choose either good or harmful actions. It is necessary to learn from the past and try not to repeat or continue the negative actions. At the same time, we should not get stuck in the past, which is completely finished. Although the karmic imprints of past actions may still be active, we have the power to influence future conditions by our present actions.

I also like to watch the science programs on TV. We are not just sending machines to Mars but staying in communication with them for months and years as they roam about digging up samples and taking pictures. I've heard scientists predicting that in the future, with global warming and population growth, living conditions will become much harder for beings on this planet. When the population is more than the planet can support, natural resources will be depleted and life will be difficult. Astronomers say that down the road, many hundred millions of years from now, our life-giving sun will destroy planet Earth in a fiery nova. A similar "end of the world" scenario was predicted by the Buddha, in the *Anguttara Nikaya*. However, in Buddhist teachings, the end of the world can never be final, because a new world is born, and the illusory life in samsara continues, through cycles of ages. Over vast spans of time, some of the ages are steeped in ignorance, while others are more favorable to receiving the light of Dharma teachings.

You may not have thought much about being born in a most fortunate time and place, unless you realize that your karma—the consequences of prior actions—could lead to being born as a nonhuman being. From a Buddhist point of view, we are living as human beings at present, but this is not our only life. There are past lives and there will be future lives. Our past lives are like yesterdays, this life is today, and future lives are our tomorrows. There is a short time between these lives called the bardo, which is much like the period of dreaming between going to sleep and waking up.

There are many realms, which are grouped into six larger categories: god (*deva*), jealous god (*asura*), human, animal, hungry ghost (*preta*), and hell realms. As humans we are closely related to and interact with the animal realm. These other realms are not part of our daily experience, but we have been in all these places in our millions and millions of past lives.

At one time or another, each of us has experienced all these types of lives in the six realms, in our countless millions of past births. The nonhuman realms of samsara are normally invisible to us, except for the animals. In addition, these realms of samsara are not the only unseen realms of existence. Tibetan tradition teaches that there are realms outside of samsara, such as the pure abodes of enlightened buddhas and bodhisattvas, realized teachers who have died but no longer return to samsara, and deities who are protectors and guides. The infinite vastness of the cosmos that exists beyond our known universe is unimaginable.

A way to think about the cycle of rebirth in samsara is that we are like travelers always moving in and out of six hotels. Each time we check into one of the hotels, we get a new room. Usually we don't remember our past hotels or rooms, thinking each time that the present one is the only one we have known. Actually, we just stay there for a little while and then check out, leaving our luggage behind.

It is amazing how technology has created a comfortable life for so many people and made wisdom teachings freely available, either directly from a teacher or through the various media. Just the ability to write is a marvelous wonder that we take for granted. Because of the human ability to write, today we can read the wisdom of the Buddha that he spoke thousands of years ago.

We are like magicians moving around the earth with our computers and cell phones. At this present time with the Internet and media technology, we are able to receive teachings from around the world while sitting in our homes. Even the death of a teacher does not stop our ability to see and hear his or her teachings, since video talks are offered to be watched or downloaded for free. We are fortunate to be alive in this time when the newest practitioner can experience teachers, both living and dead, at the click of a button or mouse. In the past, only those with great wealth, traveling fortitude, or extremely rare subtle minds could receive the Dharma directly.

Traditionally, a description of what makes up a precious human birth has eight freedoms from circumstances and ten endowments to give you a deep appreciation for being alive. These eighteen can be summed up as being born in a place and time that meets our physical needs, the Buddhist teachings are available for us to receive, and our facilities are sharp enough to understand and practice the teachings. This is what is meant when Buddhist teachers talk about having a precious human birth.

Thinking about all the good qualities of being a human is something we practice at the start of a meditation session in order to fill our minds with the resolve to take what we have been given and make it even more precious by putting it to use. Considering ourselves to be flawed and lacking in good qualities leads to problems with self-worth; it also reduces the energy we need to tackle the habitual patterns that cause us and others trouble. Without effort, it is very hard to accomplish anything.

I am very pleased to be a human being, yet I know that I can make what I have been given even better. I know I am not perfect, yet I also know I have the ability to transform my imperfections. Remembering this when I begin to practice or study makes any effort needed during the session much more freely available. Resting meditation is not just sitting on a cushion and zoning out. Contemplative Meditation is not just thinking about whatever arises in the mind. Practicing either form of meditation takes joyful exertion and self-discipline.

Think of how fortunate you are that right now you have this chance to work with your mind. When you take a joyful interest in meditation and understand the outstanding relevance of what you're doing, you won't be distracted by less important thoughts or tempted by the impulse to do unnecessary tasks. You can always

The eight eases and the ten obtainments complete a precious human body. Contemplate how difficult it is to attain a precious human body by considering the example of peas dropping over a needle and the rarity of a single pea staying on top of the needle. Contemplate the difficulty of obtaining a precious human life by considering the number of other sentient beings compared with human beings. Contemplate the difficulty of obtaining the cause of a precious human body by considering how few human beings are actually concerned with accumulating the causes of becoming a practitioner of virtue. So, at this time, having obtained this precious human rebirth just this once, without allowing it to be wasted, it is necessary to practice purely the sacred and perfectly pure sublime path of Dharma.

—THINLEY NORBU RINPOCHE, *A Cascading Waterfall of Nectar*

---

find the time for a session of meditation when you know how to arouse the intention to exert yourself.

Endowments and Freedoms of Being Human

Just having a human body alone does not automatically make a human birth "precious." Reflect on the eighteen conditions— the ten endowments and eight freedoms—of being human. The ten endowments include favorable external conditions as well as advantages that are personal to the individual. The eight freedoms entail being free from conditions that make it difficult or impossible to practice the Dharma. When we think about these states, and realize that we are free from them, it gives rise to feelings of gratitude and delight. Not only have we obtained a human birth, but we have obtained the freedoms that make our human life precious. The eight freedoms help us to practice the

Dharma, and recognizing this inspires us to make a joyful effort in practice.

The Ten Endowments

1. We have a human form, which provides the necessary supports for practicing the Dharma.
2. Our sense faculties are intact, enabling us to follow the teachings.
3. We have a wholesome lifestyle and right view.
4. We live in a place where a Buddha appeared (in our case, Shakyamuni Buddha).
5. The Buddha gave enlightened teachings, the Dharma.
6. His teachings are still available in our time.
7. Conditions favorable for practice are present.
8. We have faith in the Buddha's teaching.
9. We are able to practice the teachings.
10. We are able to receive the guidance of an authentic living teacher, or spiritual friend.

The Eight Freedoms

There is no freedom to practice the Dharma if we are born or live:

1. In a place where the Dharma teachings are unknown or unavailable.
2. With a developmental disability and without suitably sharp faculties.
3. In a land filled with proponents of wrong views such as the extremes of eternalism and nihilism. (Eternalism is the belief that things have a solid, lasting, independent existence. Nihilism is the belief that things do not really exist and have no meaning.)
4. In a dark age when not even the word "Dharma" is ever heard, because a Buddha has not come.
5. As an animal, who is subject to being preyed upon or hunted

and other severe sufferings, and who is not capable of understanding the Dharma.

6. As a long-lived god (*deva* or *asura*), a being who lives for eons without considering cause and effect and at the moment of death dies with wrong views.

7. In the hell realms, where beings repeatedly experience the sufferings of the hot and cold hells.

8. In the realm of the "hungry ghosts" (*pretas*), where beings suffer from constant hunger and thirst.

4

Visualization

Visualizing the Buddha is a source of comfort and blessings, and a way to strengthen our inner wisdom.

Visualization is a central feature of Tibetan Buddhist meditation. In Contemplative Meditation, after appreciating the human body and life that allow us to practice, we next bring the Buddha to mind by visualizing his form. This practice will help to concentrate our attention and inspire us by making us feel that we are in the presence of the enlightened qualities that we aspire to.

Shakyamuni Buddha is my hero. Since I was a boy my life has been in a close relationship with the Buddha's wisdom. Through him I have found a path to inner peace and happiness. His teachings have given me tools to work with my mind and emotions and shown me ways to look at my everyday experiences. As the years go by, the truth of what he taught becomes more and more evident. The deeper my study is, the more interesting and useful his words become to me.

Visualizing Shakyamuni Buddha, remembering his qualities, and contemplating some of his teachings is one of my favorite daily spiritual practices. To me, spiritual practice means that my mind is in line with the true nature, my thoughts are in the company of great teachers and teachings, and wholesome qualities are arising. Because I appreciate the Buddha and trust his teachings so very much, I take the time to cultivate in my heart the wish to be like him and to be helpful to others, as he is.

When we look repeatedly at a person whom we see every day, or at a photograph or an object, then it is easy to bring their image to mind. The way of visualizing in meditation is not different from this familiar way of calling an image to mind that we do regularly. Over the years, I have looked at many paintings and statues of Shakyamuni Buddha while remembering his good qualities, such as wisdom, compassion, and loving-kindness. Now I find it is easy to recall his image. If visualization does not seem so easy to you when you first start out, do not be discouraged but continue to do the practice regularly, and the clarity of the image will improve.

To help you in your visualization, it is important that you choose an image that has meaning and an energetic quality of aliveness for you. (The line drawing in this chapter is an example that you can use.) Once you have chosen your image carefully, the next step is to become familiar with it by looking closely at it again and again. This focused observation should be done by taking in the whole image. If any area is not clear, then take time to look closely at the details. In the beginning it can be helpful to spend a little time visualizing just one part of the image, like the eyebrows or hands. However, visualizing buddhas and bodhisattvas is a little different from visualizing ordinary figures, because they are not seen as solid forms.

When you visualize Shakyamuni Buddha in the space before you, he should have the quality of being transparent like a rainbow, a hologram, an illusion, or the reflection of the moon in water. We don't imagine the Buddha as an ordinary being with a solid body wearing regular clothes, nor do we see him as being flat like a picture. We imagine the Buddha's form as wisdom light. Within this wisdom light we feel that there is immeasurable compassion. This compassion is radiating out, and we try to connect with it, feel it, and experience it.

If you bring the Buddha to mind,
He will reside in your presence.
He will always grant your blessings
And will completely liberate you from all faults.

—from *The Sadhana of Shakyamuni Buddha,* translated
by Khenpo Gawang Rinpoche and Gerry Wiener

As an aid to learning visualization, you may keep a copy of the drawing of the Buddha near you during the session, to look at before starting and to refer back to during the session. Start by looking carefully at the image to help with the details of the visualization. But remember that a drawing or painting is just a symbol. The visualization should be "alive" with qualities of presence (power). It is made of light much like a rainbow. Most people experience at first that their visualization is more general than highly detailed. Just know that if you keep doing the meditation again and again, over time you will gain familiarity, connection, and clarity. Have confidence.

If you wish, you may visualize that there are many, many other buddhas, bodhisattvas, and members of the Noble Sangha surrounding Shakyamuni Buddha. For example, Avalokiteshvara, the Bodhisattva of Compassion, is visualized as luminous white in color, with one face, four arms, and two legs. As shown in the drawing on page 166, one pair of hands are joined at his heart in the gesture known as *anjali,* which symbolizes the union of compassion and emptiness. His other pair of hands hold objects: in his right hand, a crystal mala (meditation beads, used to count the number of mantra recitations), and in his left hand, a white lotus. He is seated in a full lotus posture of crossed legs with feet resting on his thighs. As with the description of Shakyamuni Buddha, Avalokiteshvara is not visualized as an ordinary being but having a wisdom light form.

In visualizing the Buddha, the emphasis is on being able to

visualize a clear image of him in front of you, *over time*. To truly feel the wisdom light of the Buddha will take some mental exertion at first. If you make this aspiration from your heart, you will connect with the omniscient and compassionate Buddha appearing in front of you through your visualization.

How to Visualize the Buddha

Visualize Shakyamuni Buddha seated in the space before you and slightly higher than your forehead. If you open your eyes and, without tilting your head, raise your gaze slightly upward into the space in front of you, this is where the Buddha would be visualized. The size of the Buddha and the distance from you is dependent upon the visualization. If you visualize the seated Buddha human-sized, then he is about six feet distant. If Buddha is visualized to fill the space in front of you like the screen at the IMAX theater, then the distance would be greater. The key point is that you can comfortably "see" the whole figure of the Buddha.

His color is a radiantly beautiful gold. He is seated on a lion throne, which is a platform held up by standing snow lions with turquoise manes. The throne is a symbol of the Buddha's sovereignty, while the snow lion is a sacred mythological animal that is the emblem of Tibet. This animal is often shown in art as leaping playfully amid the snowy peaks of Tibet's mountainous landscape. The lions represent the fearlessness and confidence of the Buddha.

On top of the lion throne is a large lotus blossom, and in its center are sun and moon discs like two large gold and silver pancakes or flat pillows. Here sits Shakyamuni Buddha clothed in the three dharma robes, which are a skirt and two shawls of a saffron color.

He is seated in the vajra position, which is upright with crossed legs and the feet resting on the thighs in full lotus position. His right hand is beautifully extended in the earth-touching gesture, resting on his knee with fingertips touching the seat. His left hand

Shakyamuni Buddha

is in the meditation gesture, palm up, curved, and resting in his lap, holding a begging bowl filled with nectar (*amrita*), which is symbolic of immortality and the blessings of the Dharma.

He is blazing with confidence, like a mountain of gold. His form is completely perfect. There is no flaw, nothing missing or incomplete.

Try to connect with the Buddha in your imagination and feel that he is actually in the space in front of you. One who is able to clearly bring Shakyamuni Buddha to mind is completely engaged in the visualization.

Make the Buddha Your Companion

It is acceptable, even commendable, to visualize that the Buddha is with you at any time during the day or night. This will help strengthen the feeling that the Buddha is present with us at all times. Traditionally students are told to visualize their teachers watching them. This can help prevent students from engaging in activities that would cause themselves or others harm and suffering. Say and do things that you would feel comfortable saying and doing in front of the Buddha and bodhisattvas. For example, if you are in the habit of thinking of them as your companions, you would not want to curse or speak harshly to someone in front of them. It is not because they would judge you or disapprove, but because they are the embodiment of compassion for all beings and you wish to become more like them.

Visualizing the Buddha to be with you at all times can be a helpful deterrent, and also can be a great source of comfort and blessings. By keeping this visualization in mind as often as possible, the habitual patterns of confusion are weakened and the patterns of wisdom are strengthened. This visualization can be particularly useful in focusing the mind and intent as preparation for Contemplative Meditation.

5

Seven Ways to Accumulate Merit

Gathering merits creates the positive energy to bring us a wise and happy life. Dedicating the merit contributes that energy toward the enlightenment of all beings.

Generally, when we want to accomplish any project, there will be difficulties and obstacles before we complete our objective. It would be helpful if we could nurture strength and good fortune. Here we will make use of seven steps, called the Seven-Branch Offering, to assure that this strength of fortune, or *merit*, will build up in ourselves.

The Seven-Branch Offering

1. Appreciating
2. Offering
3. Taking responsibility for mistakes
4. Rejoicing in the goodness of others
5. Requesting the teachings
6. Asking the teachers to remain and teach
7. Dedicating the merit to all beings

1. *Appreciating.* The first step is that we bring up a clear sense of appreciation. If we deeply appreciate the qualities of the Supreme

Teacher, the Buddha, it is an automatic remedy to our pride and arrogance. It makes us able to receive. Our receptivity is enhanced because we mentally bow; we surrender to his superiority by having a full sense of appreciation.

2. *Offering.* The second step is that we show and express that appreciation in the form of offering or gifts, whether we have them assembled physically or, in the absence of that, visualize them mentally. We include the full abundance of anything that is enjoyable, that we can imagine or bring to mind. The point is to make it a great expression of appreciation and to give it joyfully and to let go without thinking, "Oh no, I am missing this." Without any idea of loss we are able to express our appreciation through giving and to offer it to the Buddha and his superior assembly.

3. *Taking responsibility for mistakes.* The third step is to take full responsibility for our mistakes, misdeeds, and unskillful actions of the past. Whatever we have messed up, we acknowledge and we feel remorse. Not only do we recall our own unskillful and foolish misdeeds, but we also recall the errors that all sentient beings have done.

Together with all of them, we confess it and inwardly stand up and say that this was our mistake, but we are going to make it better in the future. We are able to correct, and we want to correct, our own mistakes.

4. *Rejoicing in the goodness of others.* Having then confessed and overcome all our own mistakes, the next thing to focus on is recalling all the goodness that has ever been accomplished by the bodhisattvas and all other sentient beings anywhere in this and all worlds. This recollection and rejoicing in the goodness of others train us to be immune from a very common habitual pattern. For example, when a friend has excelled at something, a sense of envy may come up and we think, "Oh, he did it better than I did." It comes with a notion of wishing this other person to fail so he wouldn't be better than us. Any sense of being

envious or feeling jealous of others leaves a very bad imprint or wound in our own mind. On the other hand, if we are able to fully rejoice in the goodness of others when they have done things really well, then we receive the merit or goodness. In this way, without doing any work except rejoicing, we get the same profit.

5. *Requesting the teachings.* Requesting the turning of the wheel of Dharma means that we ask all the buddhas and the bodhisattvas to share their higher insight, knowledge, and liberating information. We have made it our heart's concern that the Dharma be accessible to all sentient beings, and that's why we request them to teach.

6. *Asking the teachers to remain to teach.* We ask the buddhas and bodhisattvas not to disappear into a state of nirvana, but to stay in this world for the benefit of all sentient beings. We ask them to remember how much they are needed here so that they may stay longer and longer.

7. *Dedicating the merit to all beings.* The last step is to ensure that what we have done is not just for our own sake. We want to confirm that it is for the good of everyone and contributes to the enlightenment of all. Begin by imagining and recalling the goodness of all the buddhas and the bodhisattvas of the past, present, and future. Take that goodness, together with the goodness of whatever you have created, and put it all together. Then distribute and share it mentally with all sentient beings.

Note that in a Contemplative Meditation session, you will be dedicating the merit twice. The first time is the seventh step above, in which you dedicate the merit accumulated from doing the first six steps of the Seven-Branch Offering. The second time is at the end of your meditation, when you dedicate the merit accumulated from the whole session and specifically for the work done by contemplating the Four Seals.

How to Make Offerings

Traditional Tibetan offerings could be a white offering scarf called a *khata*, seven bowls of water, incense, butter lamps (candles of clarified butter instead of wax), flowers, music played on traditional Tibetan liturgical instruments, and a mandala offering which is a bottom plate with three rings and a top. The mandala rings are filled one at a time with a mixture of rice, barley, and perhaps, if the person wealthy, gems, coins, precious metals, and semiprecious stones.

The Western student could offer the same things as a Tibetan would. At Pema Karpo we offer seven bowls of fresh water, seven candles, incense, and flowers, and we have a mandala offering that stays on a side table.

Many students offer fresh water, candles, flowers, and incense regularly. They also may make lovely arrangements of crystals, precious or semiprecious gems, or seashells.

These are examples of things I have seen in monasteries, dharma centers, and people's home shrines. What Tibetans or Westerners should offer cannot be strictly specified since it all depends on the person, what they have, and what they want to offer.

Daily I offer on my shrine box seven votive candles, seven bowls of fresh water, and incense. Sometimes I add fresh flowers. This is a Tibetan-American way!

I recommend that the main practice be a visualized offering. Any object that is beautiful and precious to you can be visualized and offered. The advantage of visualized offerings is that they can fill the whole universe!

Dedicating the Merit

Dedicating the merit is like saving our work on a computer. No matter how long we work, if we have not saved our documents and the computer shuts down, we will have lost all the work. This is what happens if we do not dedicate the merit for all sentient beings. If later we become angry or have other conflicted emotions or states of mind, we will lose the wisdom, merit, and virtue we have accumulated.

When I dedicate the merit, I visualize the buddhas and bodhisattvas all gathered in front of me. They are witnessing the dedication, which is for all sentient beings of the past, present, and future. First I think to myself that in the ways these great beings dedicated the merit is the way I also offer the dedication. I dedicate the merit, wishing that the Dharma teachings may flourish in the world, that all sentient beings may have their idea of a happy and successful life with many good things, and that they may all eventually become buddhas without any suffering or confusion.

Usually I do not focus on one person or situation when I dedicate the merit. If I am asked to remember someone or to practice for someone who is dying, sick, having problems, or in need of merit, I will think of all sentient beings first and then focus on the person by name.

Dedication of merit means that we mentally gather up in our mind the goodness of ourselves and all the other sentient beings in the universe. We include the goodness that has been accomplished in the past, is being accomplished in the present, and will be accomplished in the future. Then we dedicate the goodness to the awakening of all sentient beings. When we dedicate the merit, we should think that we want to achieve the enlightened state of the Buddha in order to help all sentient beings achieve it also.

We wish that all may reach the lasting, stable happiness that is fully enlightened buddhahood. We dedicate the goodness to the world and the experience of sentient beings in such a way that there may not be any suffering through famine, catastrophe, struggle, and strife. Instead we wish there may be well-being, harmony, and peace on earth.

The dedication of all the goodness—the positive energy and

good karma—means sharing it and giving it away firstly for the supreme purpose of reaching buddhahood, the state of perfect peace, and secondly for the temporary gift of peace and freedom from suffering on our planet. We wish that the goodness helps the Buddha Dharma to endure, to be accessible to all beings, and to be a contributing factor in their achieving enlightenment.

On a daily level, we can dedicate merit by wishing that beings, wherever they are, will have immediate happiness, well-being, and freedom from the struggles of famine, sickness, war, and other forms of suffering.

Verses for Dedicating the Merit

When we speak the words of dedication, we can call to mind the presence of great teachers such as Shakyamuni Buddha to be our witness. In their enlightened presence we speak words of dedication such as these.

Simple Dedication

In the same ways that buddhas and bodhisattvas have always
    done,
I dedicate in that way.

Prayer for the Peoples of This Earth

At this very moment, may the people and nations of this
    earth
Not even hear the names of disease, famine, war, and suffer-
    ing,
But rather may pure conduct, merit, wealth, and prosperity
    increase,
And may supreme good fortune and well-being always
    arise.

Dedication of Merit

By this merit may all attain omniscience.
May it defeat the enemy, wrongdoing.
From the stormy waves of birth, old age, sickness, and death,
From the ocean of samsara, may I free all beings.

Accumulating Merits

Merits are virtuous actions that make positive imprints on our consciousness, and these imprints become the principal cause of happiness and fortune in future lives. We accumulate merit by performing positive karmic actions; we retain it by giving it away—that is, dedicating the merit for the benefit of all sentient beings.

Merit is a way we can create for ourselves the necessary situations and good luck to bring into our lives the people to help us make a wise, happy, and fulfilled life. Merit is intangible, but most of the causes and effects are tangible. There are two types of merit that we can accumulate: with a focal point and without a focal point. Merit created through using a focal point leads to good karma and happiness, in our present and future lives, in the familiar world of duality. Merit without a focal point is wisdom. To attain buddhahood we must have wisdom, which dispels ignorance and illusion so that we go beyond duality, to the experience of emptiness and nonduality. So we need both merit and wisdom—merit that produces good karma, and wisdom that paves the way to enlightenment.

There are many types of merits with a focal point that anyone can perform. Some typical merits are traditional Buddhist customs. For example, in the Tibetan culture it is believed that if you save the lives of other beings, your own life is lengthened, and if you kill sentient beings, your life will be shortened. If someone is very sick, teachers will recommend that the person save the lives of animals and free them. There are many ways we can adapt these kinds of meritorious actions for modern life in the West. (See the examples under the heading "Ways to Accumulate Merit.")

Several years ago His Holiness the Dalai Lama ordered the closing of all pig farms and chicken farms run by Tibetans in India. He saw how the poor hens were shut tightly in multilayered cages, one above the other. He even closed down the egg-laying farms, because the hens were eventually sold for slaughter. He declared that raising animals for commercial purposes is not a right livelihood. His Holiness buys animals such as sheep and lets them live till they die a natural death.

Historically Tibetans were not vegetarians because of the difficulty of growing vegetables in the conditions of their homeland. In India, the first lama from Tibet to become a vegetarian was Kyabje Chatral Rinpoche, the oldest living Dzogchen master, who turned one hundred years old in 2013. He also set an example by using donations he received to purchase live fish as they are being brought in by the fishermen and releasing them back in their habitat. Our modern economy, in which food animals and pets may be sold in places far from their normal habitats, may make it tricky to follow these examples without causing further problems for the animals or the environment. For example, we can't just release a tropical bird in a cold climate. However, at my center in Memphis, students often purchase red worms from bait shops and free them on the land in special places prepared for them.

Another traditional example of merit making in the rugged terrain of Tibet is that paths and roads are made smooth so that it is easy for animals and humans to walk or drive. This can be done anywhere, for example by removing big rocks, fallen branches, or other obstacles on the roadway or street that could cause accidents, or by filling in potholes. Helping in the cleanup after natural disasters may include this kind of merit. In our modern times, I think this merit can also include picking up litter and broken glass, and recycling discarded items.

The way to accumulate merit is to be willing to give, willing to open, willing to not hold back. . . . As a result of opening yourself, you begin to experience your world as more friendly. That is merit. You find it easier to practice the dharma, you have fewer kleshas, and circumstances seem to be hospitable.

—PEMA CHÖDRÖN, *Start Where You Are*

All beneficial activities are a way of generating merit. Merit is the antidote for negative emotions when the meritorious actions of body, speech, and mind are done with good motivation and intention. Some merits are a direct antidote and some are an indirect antidote. Merit with a focal point is an indirect antidote, since it helps to bring about the causes and conditions that lead to wisdom.

Disturbing emotions, misperceptions, and confusions are not in accord with the nature of reality. Wisdom is in accord with the nature of reality. Wisdom is the power of truth, so its very presence in the mind causes the disturbances to weaken or vanish, just as light banishes darkness as soon as we flip the switch in a dark room.

Merit is the main cause for meeting the Dharma teachings and an authentic teacher in this life. When you do find this authentic teacher, the next step is to make effort and be diligent in working with and following their advice and instructions. Again, it is merit that sets up the causes and conditions to receive and hear the teachings in a way that is beneficial to you. My root teacher would often exhort us by saying, "Dharma practice is not for the Buddha. The Buddha is already enlightened. Dharma practice is for you. It is for your benefit."

Ways to Accumulate Merit

We can accumulate merit with a focal point by doing the practices described in this book, including:

Avoid doing anything that might bring harm to others.
Make every effort not to kill any living creatures,
Birds, fish, deer, cattle, and even tiny insects,
And strive instead to save their lives,
Offering them protection from every fear.
The benefit of doing so is beyond imagining,
And the greatest ritual for the living or deceased.

—KYABJE CHATRAL RINPOCHE

√ Reading about and contemplating the Four Seals: impermanence, multiplicity, suffering, and emptiness
√ Maintaining proper meditation posture
√ Cultivating bodhichitta and compassion
√ Visualizing Shakyamuni Buddha
√ Reciting the Seven-Branch Offering
√ Chanting the Heart Sutra
√ Cultivating the six paramitas, or virtues of the bodhisattva (see page 61)
√ Contemplating sacred thoughts and objects
√ Doing meditations and prayers in order to purify any negative karma you have created

Other examples of merit with a focal point would be:

√ Freeing animals about to be killed
√ Feeding and caring for homeless or sick animals
√ Supporting no-kill animal shelters
√ Building roads and paths
√ Removing obstacles and litter
√ Helping the poor and needy
√ Helping to support Dharma activities like meditation centers, ceremonies, and the creation of statues and Dharma books
√ Public service activities related to literacy, soup kitchens, shelters, volunteering, energy conservation, recycling, etc.

6

Bodhichitta, the Awakened Heart

Awakening bodhichitta is the path of the bodhisattvas, who are great beings dedicated to benefiting others.

The last time I met with my root teacher, His Holiness Penor Rinpoche (1932–2009), was at his retreat center in upstate New York, where he had asked me to stay for a few days. He loved the United States and thought it was a great and beautiful country. I remember with great clarity a lunch we shared and how full of life and happy he was as he kept offering me more servings of food to eat.

In the early morning before I left, I went to his room and offered three prostrations and a white khata scarf—the traditional greeting between teacher and student. His Holiness said, "Are you leaving today?" I said, "Yes, I am leaving." His Holiness then advised me, "When you teach Dharma, raise compassion first and then teach. You will be beneficial." This was the last conversation we had together, and for me this was the last instruction from my teacher.

It is compassion that gives rise to bodhichitta. *Bodhichitta* may be translated as "awakened heart." Examined more deeply, it is the thought or resolution that you want to reach the complete and full enlightenment of a buddha for the sake of all sentient beings

Compassion reduces our fear, boosts our confidence, and brings us inner strength. By reducing distrust, it opens us to others and brings us a sense of connection with them and a sense of purpose and meaning to life. Compassion also gives us respite from our own difficulties.

—HIS HOLINESS THE DALAI LAMA, *Beyond Religion*

---

without exception, so that you can benefit them by helping them to reach ultimate happiness too.

Both bodhichitta and compassion are the major conditions needed to achieve stable and lasting happiness, joy, peace, and mental well-being. They both come from looking carefully at ourselves and our world and seeing how all beings are affected by suffering. No one likes or wants trouble and suffering—all beings share that in common, from the tiniest insect to the human race. We strive for happiness without knowing how to do so skillfully, and so end up in more suffering and trouble.

The type of mind training that leads to an awakened heart is entirely different from our conventional actions and expectations. All our usual concerns are about nourishing ourselves, thinking about "me" and "mine." We cherish ourselves and what we call "ours"—our life, our family and friends, our race, our nation—as being more valuable than others. That's the habitual way that most people think. Although to a great extent this attitude is encouraged by society, the fact is that having a strong habit of putting yourself first is not the way to have a happy life.

Many people argue that in order to love others, you must love yourself first. The big mind flip is the understanding: "We are all interrelated and interdependent; so if I take care of others first, there will be happiness for me and happiness for everyone else, too." This is the attitude of a person who possesses an awakened heart, the mind of bodhichitta.

To develop bodhichitta, there are several methods taught in

Buddhism. Three suggestions that can be practiced at any time are Atisha's "seven-point instruction on cause and effect," Shantideva's "sending and taking," and the four immeasurables (see "Three Ways to Arouse Bodhichitta," pages 62–68). It is not necessary to do all these methods in one session. Use whatever is the easiest way for you to arouse bodhichitta. It can be simply a brief thought such as "I am going to do this contemplation for the benefit of all sentient beings."

While my teacher told me to raise compassion before I teach, it is equally important to raise compassion before beginning a meditation session. You can even do it several times during the session. That is, arouse bodhichitta before starting the practice, renew it during the practice, and generate it again at the end of the practice. Bodhichitta is like candy—sweet at the beginning, the middle, and the end.

Bodhichitta can be classified into several types. *Relative bodhichitta* is the conventional type, which involves wanting to become a buddha in order to help all sentient beings. *Ultimate bodhichitta,* also called *absolute bodhichitta,* is the more radical type, which means having direct perception of the true nature of things, as being empty of self.

Another way of classifying bodhichitta distinguishes the wish from the action. *Aspiring bodhichitta* is the aspiration to achieve enlightenment to benefit all beings. *Entering bodhichitta* means not just aspiring to awaken but actually getting to work, by following the vows of a bodhisattva and practicing the six paramitas ("perfections" or virtues) that lead to enlightenment.

Many Westerners believe that the bodhisattva is one who vows to *postpone* his or her own enlightenment until all others are enlightened first. But actually, this is only one of three types of bodhichitta, described as the way of the king or queen, the way of the ferryman, and the way of the shepherd.

1. The *king or queen* seeks to become enlightened first, in order to lead others to enlightenment. In this way, we work to free ourselves

because the wiser, clearer, and more skillful we are, then the better able we are to help others.

2. The *ferryman* wants to achieve enlightenment along with all other beings. This person is like a boatman who ferries passengers across the ocean of samsara: everyone arrives together.

3. The *shepherd* represents the highest ideal. As the shepherd, we delay our own enlightenment in order to guide all other beings to enlightenment first, before realizing it ourselves. This means that we would put others first, before thinking of our own benefit. The reasoning is that I am one person, while sentient beings are countless. One person is much less important than limitless beings, so I work with the view of liberating all beings first.

The great example of the third attitude is the Bodhisattva of Compassion, Avalokiteshvara. First, compassion arose in him upon seeing the troubles of all sentient beings. Then, in order to liberate them, he took the bodhisattva's vow, saying that until all sentient beings attained enlightenment and were liberated, he would remain in samsara and work for their benefit and liberation.

The motivation of bodhichitta is bigger than anyone's abilities in a lifetime or even many lifetimes. Even when one is enlightened, still it won't happen instantly that all other beings become enlightened. Look at the Buddha: he himself had great bodhichitta and was enlightened, but here we are, more than twenty-five hundred years later, with limitless sentient beings still suffering in samsara.

The great mind of bodhichitta doesn't worry over the result, but instead has the motivation to make the effort, the willingness to do the necessary work, to make it happen no matter how long it takes for all beings to be enlightened.

Even when we are not enlightened and we don't have power to ease the suffering of all sentient beings, we can have great motivation and a big plan. Often His Holiness Penor Rinpoche would tell us that we have to have a big plan. Even if it is not completely accomplished in this lifetime, you will have done a lot. If you have only a small plan, then even if it is accomplished in your lifetime, it does not do much. Just as we are now, we can make a start with the right motivation: the benefit of others. Whatever we do—whether meditation or doing something helpful or virtuous—at the end of the activity we can dedicate the merit to the enlightenment of all beings.

The Six Paramitas: Virtues of the Bodhisattva

The paramitas are virtues that the bodhisattva must perfect in order to reach buddhahood. Often translated as "transcendent perfection," *paramita* literally means "gone to the other shore." This shore is our ordinary world, while the other shore is enlightenment.

1. *Generosity.* This paramita means giving in a broad sense, not just donations to the needy and offerings of food, but sharing knowledge and other kinds of help, with no expectation of return. The three main types of giving are (a) fulfilling material needs, (b) helping people to overcome fear, and (c) teaching the Dharma

2. *Discipline* or morality. Here, "discipline" refers to ethical behavior and exercising self-control. There are three types of morality: (a) refraining from harmful actions of body, speech, and mind; (b) cultivating, protecting, and increasing virtue; and (c) being of benefit to sentient beings.

3. *Patience.* There are three types of patience: (a) patience with those who harm or offend us, so that we refrain from retaliating; (b) tolerating hardship by seeing it as the result of karmic causes; and (c) persistence in studying and practicing the Dharma.

4. *Diligence* or joyful effort. There are three types of diligence: (a) armor-like diligence, which gives us the courage

and energy to persist until we achieve the goal; (b) diligence in positive actions through the practice of the paramitas; and (c) insatiable perseverance, shown by devoting all one's energy to the benefit of others.

5. *Meditative concentration.* There are two essential kinds of meditation: (a) resting meditation (shamatha) aimed at cultivating a mind that is undisturbed by distraction, and (b) special insight or analytical meditation (vipashyana) that makes it possible to gain insight into the true nature of reality.

6. *Wisdom. Prajna,* or wisdom, is the supreme knowledge of emptiness. There are three categories of Mahayana teachings on insight into the wisdom of emptiness: (a) hearing the teachings, (b) thinking about the teachings, and (c) meditating on the teachings.

Three Ways to Arouse Bodhichitta

If we use Atisha's and/or Shantideva's methods, and spend time with the four immeasurables, we allow ourselves the space to develop true bodhichitta. By developing bodhichitta, we bring ourselves and others closer to true peace and happiness.

Atisha's Seven-Point Instruction on Cause and Effect

Atisha Dipamkara (982–1054) was a great Indian master and scholar. He was the author of many texts and one of the main teachers at the famous university of Vikramashila.

1. *Mother-beings.* The first step in Atisha's method is to remember that a mother is necessary in order for any being to come into life. If we believe in rebirth, it is a process that goes on infinitely, so who can say when it all started? This is the view being expressed when it is said that at one time or another, all sentient beings have been our mother. This is why sentient beings are often

called "mother-beings." This step engenders gratefulness for the tremendous kindness these other beings have shown us by giving us our bodies.

2. *Gratitude for the kindness of others.* The second step is to remember the kindness of having been nurtured in our mother's body during pregnancy and in the world after birth. Once born, we were not left to starve or to die of cold and heat. There was someone to give us nourishment and clothing, someone who taught us to walk and talk, and how to live in the world. There have been kind people who nurtured us.

Even for those of us with a less-than-perfect childhood, someone nurtured us, at least enough so that we didn't die. In arousing bodhichitta, we need to remember the kindness of those who have taken care of us in this life and of all those caretakers in the countless lives that preceded this one. We let that awareness grow in our hearts until we feel an unmistakable sense of gratitude.

3. *Wish to repay the kindness.* The third step arises from the first two. In vividly remembering the kindness of others, we feel a compelling urge to reciprocate. We wish to do something good for those who did something good for us, in this life and in countless others—in other words, for all living beings.

4. *Desire for happiness for all.* The fourth step is feeling so friendly toward everyone that we begin wishing that they could all be happy. That feeling leads to the realization that to be truly happy, we must also know how to maintain happiness. This desire for the present and future happiness of other beings leads us to a deeper appreciation of all sentient beings.

5. *Love and compassion.* In feeling love for all beings—the wish to bring them happiness—we become intensely aware of what those beings are doing, like a mother intimately concerned with her baby's well-being and growth. This is the fifth step. We see clearly that all beings are stuck in suffering and that they are only making more trouble for themselves and for others. It's heartbreaking to witness.

A genuine wish grows in us to do something about that condition. We want to free everyone from suffering and trouble. When that attitude grows in our hearts, then self-concern will begin to fade. As you generate bodhichitta, you really want to take all that suffering from them. This is compassion.

6. *The extraordinary motivation.* The sixth step is called the extraordinary motivation or attitude. Extraordinary motivation is based on a feeling of fervent concern to free others from pain. This feeling gives way to a deep resolution that arises within us to do something about their suffering. That resolution is coupled with courage and a staunch resolve: "I have to do something myself. If necessary, I will work until all beings are freed from suffering, no matter how long it takes and even if I am the only one doing so."

7. *Awakened heart.* The final step is bodhichitta, the awakened heart. We realize that we have work to do. If we are going to free all beings from suffering and bring them permanent happiness, then we had better get in shape. The best shape to be in is fully enlightened buddhahood. So buddhahood is what we must accomplish as soon as possible. We make a steadfast vow that we will dedicate the rest of this life and all future lives to gaining enlightenment.

Sending and Taking

"Sending and taking" (*tonglen* in Tibetan) is the practice of sending our good qualities and helpfulness to others with the out-breath and taking into ourselves the problems and suffering of others with the in-breath. This method was taught by Shantideva in his *Bodhicharyavatara*.

We begin by considering thoroughly how similar we all are. Everyone wants to feel well and to avoid pain and discomfort. For Shantideva's method to work, we must accept that this basic attitude holds true for us all.

The practice of sending and taking means that we sit quietly in meditation posture and use our normal breathing in and out as a focus of attention, joining it with a wish in our hearts. As we breathe out, we wish:

> May my happiness and my good qualities flow out with my breath and make all sentient beings happy and saturated with good qualities.

When we breathe in, we wish:

> Let the discomfort, uneasiness, suffering, and pain of all sentient beings be taken away from them. May I may take the burden off their shoulders.

Breathing evenly, in and out, we sit and make these wishes.

Most of us have the attitude that we want to do things and take care of ourselves first, and then we will think about others. If we look honestly at our minds, we cherish ourselves as more valuable than others. In Shantideva's tradition this is seen as a deception. The fact that self-cherishing is stronger than other-cherishing is actually what causes our problems. Our troubles come from this attitude of seeing ourselves as so important, and from all the reactions that are based on this wrong view. When implemented and done regularly, tonglen practice is powerful enough to reverse the attitude that has literally brought us so many problems from beginningless time until the present moment.

This exchanging oneself with others needs to be real and heartfelt to work. Often it is helpful to start with some being you care for deeply, someone for whom it is easy to wish the best and feel a desire to take on their cares. Gradually you can move outward to include more and more beings until even the most dreadful being or circumstance can be a part of your practice.

Sometimes people tell me they can't do tonglen practice because they have enough of their own problems or that most people they know cause them problems. They can't imagine wanting to take on their enemies' problems or feeling love for them. Really, we do not know or come in contact with over ninety-nine percent of the human beings on even this world. We do not have a personal connection with many people. We can start with the beings we do have affection for and then enlarge our practice to include the huge numbers of beings that are unknown and neutral. When we are stable in our practice, we can start to add those whom we dislike or who have caused us harm.

All those people living in the houses you pass, in the cars next to you on the freeway, or those you see on TV, are just like you. The birds outside with their seeds, the raccoons eating dog food on the porch, or the squirrel peeking in my window, they are like us too. They want to be happy and safe, and they don't want to be caught in troubles and harmed.

Your motivation for doing Contemplative Meditation and these practices that give rise to bodhichitta should be the wish that all beings have good fortune and a happy life. Studying and practicing to help oneself is not wrong, but from a Mahayana view it is not the best motivation.

We have been thinking of "self" for a long time, and still we have a lot of suffering and trouble. We are thinking about one person's life and working to benefit one person. This is not bodhichitta. Bodhichitta is thinking of others first and wishing them to be free from suffering, and that they will discover that lasting freedom from suffering, which is enlightenment.

We are practicing for all the countless sentient beings. We are not being narrow-minded, thinking of only of ourselves or of a few people whom we love. Rather, we are thinking innumerable beings. This mindset is called the "hero's mind" or "big mind" because it has a wide view.

Sitting down and thinking, "I'm going to sit here and meditate, and then I'll feel better," is fine, but there is a better method to bring us greater happiness. All around us—among our family and friends, in our community, nation, and world—the habit pattern of complaining and finding fault abounds. Instead of focusing on our own pleasure or happiness, we could resolve to remove our misperceptions and misunderstandings through contemplative analysis and to cultivate this extraordinary attitude of bodhichitta. These practices can give us the wisdom and strength of purpose to do something about all the problems we see and hear every day. We start by having a larger motivation of whom we are going to benefit by our practice.

The Four Immeasurables

You may wish to memorize these lines and use them as contemplation and for recitation:

> May all sentient beings possess happiness and the root of
> happiness.
> May they be free from suffering and the root of suffering.
> May they not be separate from the great happiness devoid of
> suffering.
> May they dwell in great equanimity free from attachment
> and aversion, near and far.

This first line is expressing *immeasurable loving-kindness*. "May all sentient beings possess happiness and the root of happiness" asks that all sentient beings possess conditional happiness as well as the ultimate happiness, which is enlightenment.

The second line is expressing *immeasurable compassion*. Sentient beings have physical and mental suffering, and we wish them to be free of it. Then we wish them to be free from the root of suffering, which is ego-clinging and all the disturbing emotional states.

The third line is expressing *immeasurable sympathetic joy*. When all sentient beings have happiness and are free of suffering, then we will rejoice, feeling immeasurable joy.

The fourth line expresses *immeasurable equanimity*. It is the wish to be able to dwell in a great equanimity that is beyond the kinds of normal patterns found in the world. We involve ourselves constantly in pushing and pulling as we try to keep some people and situations close and push others away. Instead we want to be able to abide in the state of mind that all sentient beings have Buddha-nature, want happiness, don't want suffering, and are equally worthy of loving-kindness, compassion, and sympathetic joy.

Bodhichitta and Compassion

Bodhichitta may be translated as "awakened heart." The person whose heart is awakened wishes to achieve enlightenment for the benefit of others.

Great beings who have realized bodhichitta are called bodhisattvas. The bodhisattva ideal is the underlying motivation of practitioners of Mahayana Buddhism. A well-known Indian master, Chandrakirti, composed an homage to compassion (at the beginning of his *Madhyamakavatara,* or Entering the Middle Way), in which he said that buddhas are born from bodhisattvas, bodhisattvas are born from bodhichitta, and bodhichitta is born from compassion. In other words, we begin with compassion.

Compassion is the cause of bodhichitta. When we witness the troubles of other beings, especially when we realize that they suffer because of their confusion about the true nature of reality, we feel compassion. The attitude of compassion is soft, gentle, and caring toward sentient beings. It sees their pain very clearly and wishes to do something to ease it. From that wish grows bodhichitta, the desire to help them attain enlightenment, which means not only relieving their suffering but also leading them to the greatest happiness possible.

So, although bodhichitta is closely related to compassion, the objects of the two are different:

- The object of compassion is to free beings from suffering.
- The object of bodhichitta is to help beings attain ultimate happiness, which is enlightenment.

Part Three

The Four Seals
of the Dharma

7
The Seal of Impermanence

The nature of life is change and impermanence, yet we take what is impermanent to be permanent.

Before giving any teaching, no matter the subject, our teacher Khenchen Pema Sherab Rinpoche would start by talking about the impermanence of life. I can hear him in my mind quoting various verses by Shantideva or Nagarjuna. He was fond of describing our body as the boat that carries us across the ocean of suffering and would say that if we use it wisely we can swiftly cross to the shore of peace. He began in this way to strengthen our motivation and attention so we would focus on the teachings he was about to give. He made it personal, and that was helpful to me as a student.

The World Gets Shaky

As a student I had gained an intellectual understanding of impermanence, but it was not until April 2010 that I was shaken into understanding in a life-changing moment.

I was seated comfortably at the computer in Memphis, waiting for a Skype call from Tibet. This was the third week of giving Dharma teachings to a group of villagers from Yushu. Time was passing but no one came online for the scheduled teachings. At first I was not worried since there had been electrical problems in Yushu the night before.

Around midnight my land line rang and I was shocked to learn that an earthquake had taken place. "Half the people are dead in Yushu!" I was told. I began calling every number I had collected, but on the other end nothing worked except the phone of a small school that we support, and it just rang and rang. Staying up all night, calling repeatedly, I finally got through to the school's housefather, Ngawang. I could hear children crying loudly in the background.

"Two children are dead, two are in the hospital, and two are missing out of the total thirty-five. All the rest have injuries." Ngawang broke down in tears several times as he told the story of the earthquake. "I was inside the dining room along with most of the kids having breakfast. The cook was outside with a few children. There was a loud noise, the ground shook, and everything fell down. There was no time to run, no time to do anything. I saw a little light between two roof beams and was able to pull enough stuff away to crawl out.

"We couldn't see the kids under all the dirt and bricks, but we could hear them screaming for help. As quickly as we could, we found one after another and got them into the middle of the courtyard to safety. My greatest fear was that the little ones we had found would be hurt while we were digging for the others. We kept digging until we found the children. That was all we could do."

The next day I realized, "So this is impermanence. This is what the teachings are saying occurs all the time." Although I was spared the experience of the earthquake, my world got shaky too. When my mind had become more stable, I was able to give advice and comfort to those left in the post-earthquake rubble.

On Monday evening everything had been fine. We were sitting in front of our respective computers, chatting and laughing. By early Tuesday morning the room was destroyed and those whom I had just been talking to were now injured or dead.

Impermanence is a major part of our life. We all know this but have habitual patterns of expecting and living like we won't die soon; but who knows. There is an old Dharma saying, "We don't know which will come first, death or tomorrow." We are always in the midst of impermanence, but because we have an overlayer of confused perceptions, when we come face to face with it due to a big change, it often causes big trouble. Contemplating impermanence is not meant to depress us or cause us to live in fear but is the antidote to the "big trouble" that happens when we are caught unaware by impermanence.

We all have a general understanding of impermanence as we experience the four seasons and the years. Internalizing the meaning of impermanence is not so easy. What is easy is to try to make permanent that which is not permanent or at least feel a yearning for permanence. When we truly understand how impermanent our life is, and accept it as reality, then a great deal of suffering will automatically be removed.

Accept the Truth of Change

The easiest way to begin to internalize impermanence is to begin with time. We can think about a year and how much change occurs as we go through the seasons. Then we can think about months, weeks, days, and then one day, which has twenty-four hours to it. And within these twenty-four hours there is change, in one hour, one minute, and from one second to the next. We cannot deny there is change. The moment a second arises, it disappears. Every instant is of a fleeting nature and that's what has to be accepted.

But we don't only have to look outside. We can look at ourselves to see how our personal life has undergone so many changes from babyhood and then growing up year by year until now. We can reflect on what has happened. There has been constant change. On the Internet you can see time-lapse videos of people who filmed their face every day over a long period, showing dramatically how they changed and grew. It is amazing that technology has made it possible for anyone to discover for themselves how unstable their self-image is. But even without using technology, we can look around at the people we know and contemplate the course of their personal changing life stories.

The enjoyments of people, like the stock market, go up and down. Businesspeople may have a good profit now and maybe tomorrow already it's down the drain. The wealth, fame, glory, and strength of people is always changing, going up and down. If we take note of the news and of everyday life, we will become aware of those changes. We can broaden the vision of impermanence by considering the ever-changing planet, solar system, galaxy, and universe.

Teachers, friends, and parents—no matter how much you wish they would stay and live longer—will come to a time of passing away. In our relative reality this is the way things are. As the Buddha said, "All compounded things are subject to change and decay." Compounded things—which are just an assemblage of multiple parts—come together, remain for a time, and then disperse. This happens whether you accept and understand it or not. Sooner or later, what is born will die. There is no place to hide from this reality. No worldly quality can help.

Look at flowers, trees, animals, houses, even rocks and mountains. All things age, wear away, break down, and change. Why would a human be any different? Next time you buy flowers, think about this. No matter how much you want them to stay fresh and strong, they will soon wilt, rot, and decay.

One time I bought a beautiful fresh flower to offer at a feast. I put it in a lovely vase on the shrine. Each day I watched it droop a little more; the petals fell off one or two at a time, and the stem began to rot. I realized it was not only a beautiful flower; it was also a beautiful example of impermanence, because its freshness and perfection pass so quickly, right in front of our eyes. Think of a rose in your garden. The rose is one of the most delightful of blossoms, and also one that fades fast. Poets often liken it to the fleeting nature of life and physical beauty.

The same is true of our body. We need not feel sad or downhearted about it. This is how everything, absolutely everything, exists. Why should we resist this undeniable truth, or feel as if the universe is somehow abusing us, when what is happening is the fundamental nature of existence?

All of life and its experiences are brought together by "causes and conditions," in the chain of cause and effect that is the law of nature. Everything automatically will change and come to an end. When we are not aware of change, then automatically, due to strong habitual patterns common in human beings, we will act and react as though phenomena are lasting. When they don't last, there's disappointment, and there may be pain and suffering that can go on a long time.

Becoming aware of change down to the small details has great benefit. If we think about it and accept this truth, then when it comes to us, it will not be as painful. When ones we love and care about die, we feel unhappy. If we understand the truth of impermanence, then the shock and inability to accept the loss will be lessened or even removed. By being aware of impermanence, we are saved a lot of problems and suffering.

Even the great teachers sooner or later will come to the moment of death and leave this life. Projects and activities have a beginning and an end, no matter how much effort you put into them. They come together and then they fall apart. The successes, the obstacles, the beginnings, the endings, the changes, all show impermanence. Death usually does not wait until we have neatly finished all our projects but can take us away unexpectedly at any moment.

The Passing of a Great Teacher

Like most spiritual practitioners, I have a hero, someone who is a role model and trusted spiritual friend. My hero was His Holiness

Penor Rinpoche, eleventh throne-holder of the Palyul lineage of the Nyingma school. I first met him in Bodhgaya, the place where the Buddha was enlightened, when he allowed me to come and study at his monastery in South India. All of my good qualities from spiritual practice come from his kindness.

His Holiness Penor Rinpoche entered the final section of meditation—accomplished by great masters at the moment the breathing stops—at 8:20 P.M. on Friday, March 27, 2009, at the Namdroling Monastery in Bylakuppe, in South India. I was not at the monastery when he died, but I knew he was very ill and close to death. I received a phone call from a friend at the monastery telling me that His Holiness had passed away.

Immediately memories came to mind of the almost ten years I spent with him. There was one time at the monastery, when he was building huge statues of Shakyamuni Buddha, Buddha Amitayus (Buddha of Infinite Life), and Padmasambhava (the Indian master who brought Buddhism to Tibet in the eighth century C.E.), that a few of us monks spent all day sitting around him on the floor in his room helping with preparations. He had a box filled with special substances from Tibet and was going to put a little of them into each statue. He was going through the little box, picking things out with one hand, eating a snack with the other hand, and meeting village people who were always coming to him for advice and blessings. This was how His Holiness lived.

When His Holiness passed away, for eight days he remained in *tukdam*, a state in which the mind remains in meditational absorption even after the physical body has died. On the eighth day I arrived at Namdroling Monastery to join with students from all over the world.

Everyone was telling about the miracles that had occurred in the eight days. As the ghee in the butter lamps in his room cooled, flower petals formed. Circular rainbows were seen by all around the temple where his body remained (several photos and videos of them were posted online). The whole monastery was filled with a

When we remember that things are impermanent, we are less likely to be enslaved by assumptions, rigid beliefs (both religious and secular), value systems, or blind faith. Such awareness prevents us from getting caught up in all kinds of personal, political, and relationship dramas.

—DZONGSAR JAMYANG KHYENTSE, *What Makes You Not a Buddhist*

---

fragrance like incense for many days, and a great peaceful feeling of his presence was there.

All his students developed great confidence in the truth of the Dharma and of his profound realization of the true nature of reality. We rejoiced in being his students, and the gratefulness that arose in our hearts lightened our sadness at his passing.

Most people at some point will personally experience a life-changing moment taking the form of a phone call, a news flash, an accident, a lab report, and the like. When someone we care about deeply dies or when changes occur unexpectedly, there is sadness and grief. A time of mourning comes to everyone in one form or another. When this arises in our lives, we can look at it as impermanence, and this will help acceptance and understanding to arise in our minds and to give us some peace.

8

The Seal of Multiplicity

Everything that exists is composed of a multiplicity of ever-changing parts, yet we believe that we are a unified whole.

European scientists announced a big step recently in the quest of science to solve the mysteries of the universe: the discovery of a subatomic particle they call the Higgs boson. Unless you are a physicist, trying to picture a subatomic particle is strange. Even stranger is trying to imagine that these incredibly tiny bits of matter themselves decay into still smaller elementary particles. This is multiplicity: the fact that everything that exists in this phenomenal universe—including you and me—is made up of components. Nothing is singular; everything is made up of parts. Despite this truth, we take for granted that things and beings—including ourselves—have a singular, permanent, solid existence that is independent and separate from other things. This is an illusion.

One time I was speaking on the phone with a young nephew who, at his monastery, had started to study a part of Buddhist literature called Abhidharma, which is a detailed analysis of psychological and physical phenomena. When I asked him how the study was going, he said it was very difficult. To make it more understandable, I told him that Abhidharma is simply "the study of you." If you have ever observed different things about what you call yourself—your body or mind—then you already know something about Abhidharma, because it is the study of the multiplicity of components that gives us the illusion of existing as a separate self that we call "I" or "me."

Multiplicity is sometimes called "compoundedness," so that "compounded things," a common Buddhist expression, means things made up of multiple components. Things that are compounded—in other words, all phenomena—have no inherent existence apart from their components, which are impermanent.

As we see with subatomic particles, all things can be broken down into smaller and smaller elements, but Buddhism divides this multiplicity into five main groups, called *skandhas* in Sanskrit, literally "heaps." So you are five skandhas put together. If you analyze any part of your body or any aspect of your mind, you can place it into one of these five heaps:

1. *Form* includes all material things and elements of the physical body, the sense organs, and any objects that can be contacted by the sense organs.
2. *Feeling* is a way of reacting to things you perceive with your senses—generally, a feeling of happiness or pleasure if you perceive the thing as pleasant, unhappiness or pain if it is unpleasant, or neutral if you are indifferent toward it.
3. *Perception* is recognizing the features of an object (shape, color, etc.), giving it a name, and forming concepts, views, and opinions about it.
4. *Mental formations* are all types of thoughts and emotions, divided into ten neutral, eleven virtuous, and twenty-six nonvirtuous mental states, plus four variable motivations. Briefly, virtuous states lead to happiness while nonvirtuous states lead to suffering.
5. *Consciousness* includes eight types of awareness: the six sense-consciousnesses (the five senses such as eye-consciousness,

ear-consciousness, etc., plus mental consciousness, or mind); the klesha consciousness, and the storehouse consciousness (*alaya*).

So *you* are these five groups put together—and that is all. There is no "I" that exists behind the five groups. But when the five skandhas come together, they produce the sense of a "self." We get attached to the five skandhas, because we identify them as "I." This is known as ego-clinging, which leads to suffering. In contemplating the Four Seals, we will be using the skandhas as a tool for examining our body and mind in order to investigate whether we can actually find the existence of a real entity called "I."

Is the Self an Illusion?

There are two kinds of truth: conventional and ultimate— also called relative truth and absolute truth. In terms of relative truth, which is our conventional, dualistic view of reality, we do have a self; it's not that we are hallucinating. But our "I" is an illusion in the sense that it has no separate, independent existence as we imagine it to have. It is not "self-existent."

The relative existence of "I" arises only in relation to the presence of the five skandhas and in connection with causes from the past and conditions. It can be considered "real" only in interrelationship with other things, just as a shadow exists only in relation to light. That is how Buddhism defines reality. Things that are dependent on other things cannot be called self-existent. Things that are impermanent cannot be real or true.

Thus it is said that there is "no self" or that all phenomena are empty of self. From the view of ultimate truth, the only reality is the unchanging fundamental nature, as it is, unmade and uncreated.

The First Skandha: Multiplicity of Form

The first skandha is multiplicity of form, which includes the elements that compose the physical body, as well as the senses and sense objects. The easiest way to begin considering form is by contemplating something very close and important to you: your body. When we investigate carefully, mentally peeling back the layers of the body like an onion, we realize that there is nothing at the center: there is actually no solid, unchanging body apart from the changing components that it is made of. In that sense, the body is not truly existent.

A scientist could tell you how every organ of the body (except for parts of the brain) replaces its cells at regular intervals. The skin, for example, changes its outer layer about every two weeks. When you think carefully about how the body is in a constant state of flux as old cells are regenerated, it becomes clear that the body is not a permanent entity.

Instead of an onion, the ancient Dharma texts from India use the banana tree as a comparison, because like our body it appears to be substantial, but if you remove all the fibrous layers of the trunk, one by one, you discover that there is no solid core. Where is the "tree," then? It is just a collection of parts that have no meaning separate from their relationship with each other. Once you take them apart, whether actually or by mental analysis, there is no basis for becoming attached to the idea of the "banana tree." That is why Jamgon Mipham Rinpoche says:

When you see feeling as water bubbles,
Perception like a mirage,
Formation like a banana tree,
And consciousness like an illusion,
They will not give rise to attachment.

Most of us hold a mental image of our physical form, seeing it as one single thing—"my body." In reality, the body is not one but a multitude of different organs, systems, and physiological events. There are the systems such as the circulatory, digestive, endocrine, musculoskeletal, nervous, reproductive, and respiratory systems. There are numerous organs, such as the brain, heart, lungs, intestines, bladder, skin, and so forth. There are the elements that make up most of our body: oxygen, carbon, hydrogen, nitrogen, calcium, and phosphorus. Can you say that any one of these components is "I"? No, only when they come together under the right conditions is there a living, breathing person with your name and address.

A traditional way of analyzing the body is by the five elements of ancient philosophies: earth, water, fire, air, and space. With the development of modern chemistry, scientists dismissed this classification, yet gradually the five elements have gained recognition in the West, now that traditional medicine is accepted as a complementary therapy. The earth element rules all the body's organs that are solid, such as flesh and bones. The water element governs the fluid components, such as blood and lymph. Fire is the heat of digestion and the processes of transformation, such as the absorption of food. The air element is respiration as well as the motion of the limbs and inner movements, including the flow of vital energies or "winds" through the subtle channels. The space element is the cavities and the hollow organs in the body. Space contains the other four elements. According to the Tibetan analysis of the dying process, the mind gradually separates from the body as the energy of the four elements dissolves. When all these components have separated and dissolved, the mind in most cases will proceed to take rebirth.

Contemplative Meditation calls for detailed self-observation. We focus carefully and keep refining our awareness by asking: where is this body and "me," where is this concern or holding on located, and where does it start and stop? Our belief that we are the body is not really graspable, definable, or locatable.

Initially we will go through these steps of analysis and refining our focus, but it won't do much to change our ego-clinging, the habit of grasping at what is perceived as "me" and "mine." This habit of desire and holding on is very strong.

But if we can manage to stay with this contemplation for a while, returning to it again and again, we will notice that this misperception of a singular solid "I" gradually becomes weaker and weaker until it fades out. At that time we should stay in this certainty that we have established. Resting in this state of understanding is Contemplative Meditation.

Seeing clearly brings certainty that there is no essential body, just as with the banana tree or the onion. Certainty does not happen by wishing or hoping. We have to look carefully again and again, day after day—turning the wheel of investigation again and again—until the habitual patterns of solidity dissolve, leaving the truth of how it is with all forms in the universe. Everything is made up of ever-changing parts.

When your mind's understanding of your body gets closer and closer to the truth, the mind will begin to be calmer and have less mental stress and emotional upheavals.

The Second Skandha: Multiplicity of Feelings

When our senses make contact with an object, one of three basic kinds of response arises: a pleasant or unpleasant feeling (pleasure or pain), or a neutral sensation.

Sentient beings are generally motivated by achieving pleasurable sensations and avoiding unpleasant sensations. When you turn on the kitchen light at night and see a big bug running toward you, it is not trying to scare you—it just wants to escape the harsh light and rush to a safe, dark, pleasant place. Even the tiniest ants that we see rushing about so busily and the worms slowly crawling through the garden soil are striving to achieve the sense experiences that they perceive as pleasant in their world. All beings consider unpleasantness as something to be avoided.

An extraordinary thing about being human is that we actually have the capacity to intentionally produce the causes of pleasure and happiness. Yet if we don't give mindful attention to what we are doing, our actions can have just the opposite effect, so that we end up doing things that cause unpleasant experiences.

A common example is that when people feel frustrated, depressed, or anxious, they may try to comfort themselves by drinking alcohol or eating too many sweets, or they may try to let off tension by snapping at someone. But such actions, instead of making them feel better, usually hurt them or their loved ones. Out of confusion and ignorance about the nature of cause and effect, along with the force of habitual behavior patterns, they apply the wrong technique to achieve pleasure and end up causing more problems.

In addition to analyzing unpleasant sensations and their causes, we must also notice the pleasant sensations, such as pleasure and happiness, and their causes. These causes are often referred to as virtues or right actions in Dharma texts. Virtuous, skillful actions produce a lasting benefit for our own "stream of experience" as it moves through this lifetime and then on to the next. Our virtuous actions usually produce benefit for others, too.

Although going toward the pleasant is natural, it is not necessarily the way to happiness. Whether pleasant or unpleasant, experiences should not be grabbed, pushed away, or ignored, because this makes ego-clinging worse and causes us to suffer. Feelings and sensations are part of life to be experienced with a gentle, open mind. We do not need to act on them in unskillful ways, but we should recognize them and allow them to be felt.

I recall walking in a local park close to my home surrounded by sweet smells and the singing of birds. Spring in Memphis is very beautiful, filled with blooming flowers, bushes, and trees. The sun was shining, the temperature was perfect, and the path was well kept and gently curving. I thoroughly enjoyed the walk in the park. We seem to spend most of our life chasing pleasurable sensations, yet often we do not experience the pleasures our five senses are offering in the present moment. We are too busy thinking or projecting ourselves into the past or future. This world can offer lavish gifts to our senses if we are open and present to experience them—and if our negative habit patterns do not get in the way.

Each time we repeat the same reaction to a situation—whether it is attraction/passion, aversion/aggression, or indifference/confusion—the impression on the mind becomes reinforced. That is why wishing and hoping that things will change is not enough to remove our problematic habitual patterns, because they have been created and strengthened by previous sensations and feelings in a karmic chain of cause and effect. Through contemplation we can begin to notice the dynamics, triggers, and roots of these patterns. If we watch our feelings carefully with mindfulness, we will see our habitual reactions and recognize which ones are truly helpful and which ones are not helping us solve our problems. That recognition doesn't mean that we will be immediately able to stop our reactivity or change our habitual choices, but just observing them is a big first step toward change. By observing ourselves with a light touch and sense of humor, without being judgmental, we may discover strengths and good qualities of ourselves we never noticed before, along with weaknesses and problematic parts.

The skandha of feeling should be noticed and recognized when it arises. However, it is hard to separate the emotions that arise from this omnipresent response of pleasant, unpleasant, or neutral, because they arise together. The feelings of the second skandha—both physical and mental—are like continuous bubbles coming up—and *pop-pop-pop,* they are gone. Contemplation brings us to a place of certainty that we have ever-changing multichannel multimedia experience going on in every moment of our lives. There is no one single solid feeling, because our feelings and sensations are a series of constantly changing mental events. When we fully realize this, when we come to that certainty, then we can stop contemplating and rest in the state without thinking analytically about the topic anymore.

The Third Skandha: Multiplicity of Perception

Perception is mental, although we perceive both physical and mental things. A concept is an idea conceived in the mind. We form an abstract idea of an object by mentally combining all of its characteristics. The concept is then our own personal mental view, attitude, or opinion. The inner conversations that go on in our mind usually revolve around such conceptualizations and subjective opinions. Sometimes it is helpful to think about the qualities of our mind in a neutral or analytical way.

This sounds rather dry until we get very angry about a situation or at a person. Later, as we chew on the incident over and over in our mind, we can hear every word and recall vividly every little nuance of the situation. If we can remind ourselves that everything happening in our mind and body is a concept or a reaction to a concept, it can help decrease the intensity of such moments of anger.

Even after the dispute is long over, we keep going over the mental concepts we formed about it, making our body tense and raising our blood pressure, and we may even end up engaging in actions that will only lead to more trouble.

A proverb of East Tibet says, "Thirty people, thirty opinions." We not only disagree with each other's opinions, but we often disagree with ourselves, since we may change our own views. The uncountable multitude of "my" opinions feeds the arguments, conflicts, and wars that cause suffering in our world. The emotional charge that we, as individuals and groups, attach to opinions can be very strong and long-lasting. The next step is to convince ourselves that what is "mine"—my life, my family, my business, my views, my politics—is more important than what belongs to others. Just think of all the problems that stem from differing political, religious, cultural, or other belief systems—all of it based on conceptual thinking.

What if we could free ourselves from a lot of distress just by changing our concepts and perceptions? By that I don't mean giving up our values or convictions, but rather "reframing" the way we interpret the situations that habitually disturb us.

On a trip to Tibet some years ago, I met a wonderful old yogi, Pema Dorje. He has lived most of his life on retreat. In the early 1960s he was captured by the Chinese during the beginning of their occupation of Tibet. For many years he was held in a "re-education" camp, where he was beaten regularly. Recalling those times, Pema Dorje gave me this valuable advice: "I took it as an opportunity to remember what my teachers taught me and to think, 'All this hardship and these beatings are purifying the aftereffects of my evil deeds from the past.'" Not only did he never get angry with the torturers, but he even said, "Those people were my spiritual teachers. They helped me to purify my karma." This is an extraordinary example of eliminating suffering by changing one's way of perceiving things. But even ordinary people can learn from it.

We have all heard the analogy about looking at the glass as either half full or half empty. It is something to consider carefully in our daily life. Just by changing concepts we can easily have more trouble or less. Sometimes you might catch yourself thinking, "This world of samsara is an unending cycle of horrible suffering!" At that moment you could remind yourself, "Right now I am in the human world. And compared with any other realm of existence, I am very well off. I don't have more suffering than I can bear. Plus I have intelligence and access to the liberating knowledge of the Dharma and the opportunity to practice. What incredible good fortune!"

So, the way we perceive and conceptualize things will determine the way we experience them. Right thinking or right concepts lead to a happy life. Negative and confused thinking and biased concepts could literally destroy a life. His Holiness Penor Rinpoche often said, "Stop remembering your problems over and over again. It's not helpful."

A funny story told to me when I was young illustrates how our mental concepts affect the way we interpret reality. There was a man who felt so bad that he decided to kill himself by jumping from the roof of a house on the edge of a cliff. As he stood at the edge getting ready to jump, he suddenly saw, way down below him, an armless man—dancing! He realized that, physically at least, he was much better off than the armless man. If a man with no arms could be dancing, why should he kill himself? His problems were not that bad. He changed his mind, climbed off the roof, and went home with a different mental attitude. Later on, he found the armless man and asked him what had made him so happy that he was dancing that day. The man replied, "Dancing? I wasn't dancing. A bug was biting my bottom and I was trying to shake it off!"

Depression and other mental disorders, and trauma from violence and abuse, can often require therapy and intervention. I do not wish to imply that all problems will just vanish magically if we change our conceptual ways of thinking, but I am saying it can help.

For most of us who are not dealing with extremely stressful mental and physical situations, taking a long, clear look at our conceptual patterns and thinking about how we might look at the meaning of life with fresh eyes and a positive attitude can lead to a more relaxed, happy, less worried outlook. If we accept our life and appreciate what we have, by removing or lessening confused or rigid concepts, then our life becomes more hopeful, and we get more energy for Dharma practice and benefiting others.

The Fourth Skandha: Multiplicity of Mental Formations

Most people make an effort to learn a trade or an art, or master a profession, in order to live comfortably and better themselves. In our materialistic world it is easy to overlook the fact that we might need to put just as much effort—or maybe more—into understanding ourselves and finding the way to inner happiness.

When I began to study the mind, I became fascinated by its complexities and potentials. In the Mahayana tradition, Buddhist psychology—the body of teachings called Abhidharma—has identified fifty-one mental states or "formations," which are divided into ten neutral, eleven virtuous, and twenty-six nonvirtuous mental states, along with four variable mental factors linked with motivation and intention. The ten neutral mental factors are in themselves neither virtuous nor nonvirtuous but can arise with either state. Whether we call them formations, factors, states, or events, the important point is that everyone is born with these fifty-one mental factors, although each person has a different combination of them.

Why study the mind in such detail? So that we can contemplate what we need to accept and what we need to reject. Which mental states or factors bring unhappiness, trouble, and suffering? Which bring happiness, peace, loving-kindness, and compassion?

The former we are calling "nonvirtuous," while the latter are called "virtuous." These traditional terms are not meant to reflect any judgment of being good or bad, right or wrong, saintly or sinful. Some translators use "wholesome" and "unwholesome," or "skillful" and "unskillful," in order to avoid such connotations. What we should focus on is that a goal of Dharma practice is to increase and make stronger the virtuous mental states. In observing our mental life, we need to know what to look for, accept, and strengthen in ourselves.

A person who is able to awaken and strengthen virtuous states is automatically going to be happier, more relaxed, and more flexible, and will naturally find more satisfaction in life. Nonvirtuous mental states increase the chances of having an unhappy life. Because of this outcome, we need to decrease nonvirtuous mental states until we are able to abandon them completely.

Everyone has heard the terms "good karma" and "bad karma." Strengthening the eleven virtuous mental states naturally leads to the actions of body and speech that cause positive or good karma,

The Root Cause of Karma

When we see how much pain and suffering our self-clinging causes, we may feel a sense of guilt, regret, or blame. It's important to look at this carefully. To truly understand karma, the words *guilt*, *regret*, and *blame* aren't necessary; we need only know its cause. The root cause of karma is ignorance—and acting out of ignorance was not our intention. If we intended to be ignorant and generate suffering, there might be something to blame or regret. But exactly whom are we going to burn at the stake?

—HER EMINENCE JETSUN KHANDRO RINPOCHE,
This Precious Life

---

which leads to peace and happiness. Strengthening the twenty-six nonvirtuous mental states does the opposite, leading to actions of body and speech that cause suffering and harm to ourselves and others, making bad karma.

Karma does not mean that we are predestined to act out our lives from these fifty-one mental factors. We can use our mindfulness and awareness to recognize them in ourselves. Recognizing them, we can systematically begin to feed the positive ones and starve the non-positive ones. This is how Dharma practice is integrated into our daily life and ordinary experience.

Eleven Virtuous Mental Formations

There are eleven virtuous formations that are positive, skillful mental states producing happiness.

1. *Faith* is of two types. One is an unexamined belief in something, the condition often called blind faith. Buddhism does not encourage this variety of belief. B. Alan Wallace expresses this well in one of his books: "The Buddha never demanded that his followers

believe anything he said. All that is traditionally required of students of Buddhism is to be open-minded, perceptive, and devoted to seeking liberation through the cultivation of insight and understanding." This kind of openness helps us develop the second type of faith, which is a natural consequence of knowing the qualities of the object of your faith. Based on knowing, this intelligent variety of faith or trust is the seed of all virtues.

2. *Conscientiousness,* or being careful, is the mindful caution that leads us to notice, and care about, the positive qualities to be adopted and the negative qualities to be abandoned. Conscientiousness makes us beware of the risks of samsara, so that we try not to fall into those traps. Instead, we try to adopt a lifestyle that leads in the direction of nirvana, the peaceful state beyond suffering.

3. *Pliancy* or flexibility can refer to the body or to the mind. Just as we can do many things with a supple, well-trained body, so with a pliant mind we can accomplish anything we want because it is completely flexible. If we want our mind to move, it will move straight ahead like an arrow. If we want our mind to rest, it will rest like a mountain. Unlike body and speech, the mind has qualities that are limitless.

4. *Equanimity* is an evenness of mind in which there is no chance for disturbances to arise. Free from all types of mental afflictions, such as anger, aversion, attachment, indifference, or confusion, the mind is able to rest naturally without being caught in attachment or aversion.

5. *Embarrassment* is sometimes an unpleasant experience, but if you think of it in the sense of conscience, it often has the good effect of holding you back from doing something negative, unskillful, or harmful, according to your own values and standards or your knowledge of the Dharma.

6. *Shame* is a healthy result of positive community standards, opinions, and evaluations. We are held back from doing harmful actions because we do not wish to be judged negatively by others. This is not the "toxic shame" that comes from abuse.

7. *Nonattachment* is a state in which we do not cling excessively to people and material things. Because we are more content, we are less likely to engage in negative actions that can come from too much attachment.

8. *Freedom from aversion* means not hating things or sentient beings, and not being upset or repelled by anything.

9. *Freedom from delusion* is a state of clarity that is the opposite of ignorance. As a result of having investigated carefully, we know what virtues to cultivate and what nonvirtues to avoid.

10. *Nonviolence* comes with being free of aggression and having a compassionate attitude toward other sentient beings, so that we avoid causing harm.

11. *Diligence* is both persistence of effort and taking delight in opportunities to do something good. Diligence enables us to perform skillful positive actions. Making effort for a negative purpose, by this definition, would not qualify as diligence. All positivity that can be achieved is achieved by joyful effort.

Ten Neutral Mental Formations

There are ten neutral formations that are always present, but under certain circumstances they may become positive or negative. While these mental formations are found, the category of neutral mental factors does not appear in traditional Abhidharma study. However, I find that using a neutral category helps students to better understand the following ten mental factors that are neither virtuous nor nonvirtuous. The ten neutral formations are the five *omnipresent* mental factors and the five *object-determining* mental factors.

Five Omnipresent Mental Factors

The five omnipresent mental factors are always present in every moment of mental activity, but we usually don't notice them:

1. *Attraction* arises on first perceiving or becoming aware of an object.

2. *Feeling* consists of physical or mental sensations of pleasure, pain, or neutrality toward an object.
3. *Perception* produces a mental concept or opinion of an object.
4. *Attention* leads to substantiation and affirmation of the object.
5. *Contact* occurs between a sense organ and an object.

Five Object-Determining Mental Factors

The five object-determining mental factors are intention, interest, remembering, focused concentration, and discriminating knowledge:

6. *Intention* is the motivation to move in a desired direction, as when we establish a goal. It is the energy that fuels our diligence. Bodhichitta is an example of intention.
7. *Interest* is what keeps the perceiving mind from moving to another object. With interest there is a holding on to the object and not letting the awareness be distracted.
8. *Remembering* or recollection is not forgetting what we already know. This helps inhibit distraction.
9. *Focused concentration* is being able to stay one-pointedly on the object being examined.
10. *Discriminating knowledge* is the ability to examine an object of perception to rid oneself of uncertainty or doubt. There are generally two types of discriminating knowledge: innate and acquired. By birth some people are specially gifted. Even from a young age, they know with certainty what their goals are and have extraordinary abilities. The acquired type of discriminating knowledge is achieved by making an effort to learn.

Four Variable Mental Formations

There are four mental factors that can have virtuous, nonvirtuous, or neutral results, depending on how they are linked with motivation and intention. These are sleep, regret, conception, and discernment.

1. *Sleep* is a state in which the senses cease their investigation because the perceiving consciousnesses are withdrawn into the storehouse consciousness, where impressions of our past actions leave their imprint. All sense of time is lost while the body rests and renews itself. Since sleep belongs to this category of variable factors, it can have either a positive or negative quality. If we fall asleep with negative intentions, then our dreams will likely include negative actions. If we fall asleep with positive intentions, our sleep will likely include positive actions. We can use our dream time to practice and generate merit.

An interesting thing happened when I was a teenager. I hadn't yet started my deep study of Buddhism, but I had memorized liturgical texts and did practices. I had a practice I did every day for one hour. It was very important, when we were given a practice, to do it every day without fail. I was strongly committed and tried to perform it daily. But sometimes I was too busy to do the practice. On those days, and only those days, at night while I slept, the practice would arise clearly in my dream, and I would do it from beginning to end, exactly as I performed it while awake.

2. *Regret* occurs when something we did fails to meet our own approval. Regret is positive if we feel sorry about something negative that we did. But if we regret doing a positive action, then our regret is negative.

3. *Conception,* or examination, is a faculty that perceives vague characteristics without details, much as when an object is seen from a distance. Conception is distinguished from the fourth variable factor, discernment.

4. *Discernment* is a thorough investigation of the characteristics of an object. There is more detail to the impression. Whether coarse and blurred or more detailed, this mental state is not positive or negative. It all depends on the linkage to other negative or positive mental events.

Sleep, Dreams, and Death

When the "gates" of the five senses are closed, the world of our experience disappears for the time we are asleep. In that regard, our sleep is very similar to our personal death. In the first moments of sleep we are overwhelmed by complete blackness, just as the mind falls into unconsciousness at death. In deep sleep there are no appearances at all. Shortly afterward, forms arise as dream images, mostly drawn from daily experiences. Imprints of previous actions feed the new ideas and pictures that emerge from the storehouse consciousness as dreams.

These stored experiences arising in a new form as dreams are like the experiences of the bardo, the state of existence between death and the next rebirth. Just as most dreamers are not aware that they are dreaming, people who have just died may not realize at first that they are dead. Therefore, many Dharma practitioners use lucid dreaming, or dream yoga, as training for their inevitable death, so that they will be able to meet the appearances arising in the bardo with awareness, knowing that any frightening images are due to their own mental perceptions. Being aware in the bardo, you can be free from fear, just like someone who lucid-dreams during a nightmare. You can exercise the intention to achieve a positive rebirth or potentially even reach enlightenment. Those who remain confused in the bardo will be "driven by the winds of karma," and their negative actions could automatically lead them to take birth in the unfavorable lower realms.

By entering the bardo with positive motivations, you can change the rebirth that will be taken. It is very important just before dying to make a mental intention to be reborn as a human being who benefits others, or to invoke the name of Amitabha, the Buddha of Infinite Light who vowed to liberate all beings in his blissful pureland. By doing this, you will set up conditions for a favorable rebirth. Even if you don't have enough merit and good karma to be reborn so favorably, it can make the difference.

I was told about a wise old master being held in one of the Chinese prison camps of the 1960s. A man in the cell next to his called out in the night, "Lama Ngasung, help me, I am dying. What should I do?" Lama Ngasung called back to him, "Remember the Buddha Amitabha. He is in the west and is red." The lama had given him the instructions for recognizing the path of light that leads to the Blissful Pureland of the Buddha of Infinite Light. In the morning the man was dead.

Nonvirtuous Mental Formations

The nonvirtuous mental formations consist of two groups: the six root kleshas and the twenty subsidiary kleshas. We are accustomed to the disturbing emotions called kleshas and consider them a "normal" part of daily life. But according to Buddhist teachings, they are in no way a part of our true nature. These kleshas are the cause of suffering, destroying our inner and outer peace.

Kleshas: Disturbing Mental States
SIX ROOT KLESHAS

"Disturbing emotion" or "disturbing mental state" is a translation of the word *klesha*, from the Sanskrit *klish*, which means to bother or disturb. Various translators render *klesha* in different ways. They are called "afflictions" or "afflictive emotions" because they afflict us with suffering. They are called "obscurations" because they conceal and cover over the pure fundamental nature of our mind. "Poison" is another translation, because the kleshas are toxic emotions and thoughts that ruin our relationships and our health. Many translators refer to them as emotions, but "mental states" or "mental factors" may be more accurate since some of them are more related to thought than to emotion. Here we are using the Sanskrit term *klesha* to avoid confusion among all the English variations.

The six principal or "root" kleshas are ignorance (unawareness of true reality), desire (clinging, attachment), anger, pride, doubt, and wrong views. They are the root of all suffering and dissatisfaction.

1. *Ignorance* is the first and most basic klesha, the origin of all troubles. Another good translation for this klesha is "confusion," which avoids some of the unrelated ideas people may associate with the English word "ignorance." The Buddhist meaning of "ignorance" has nothing to do with being uneducated or unintelligent; rather it is ignoring or being unaware of the truth, failing to understand the causes and effects of our actions. All the unskillful and disturbing states we may experience have their basis in this confusion, this unawareness. How can we realize true reality if we are confused about what is really happening from moment to moment?

There are two types of unawareness: (a) *co-emergent unawareness* means that we are endowed with it right from the moment our life begins; (b) *conceptual unawareness* is based on co-emergent unawareness but is acquired later. In the latter type we develop ideas and concepts that are not in accordance with true reality. Examples of conceptual unawareness are the belief that there is a lasting personal self or the view that after death everything is finished, without any continuation of our stream of experience. Another example is when we think that our negative emotions are not a problem but are personality traits that demonstrate our strength or determination.

2. *Desire*, the next root disturbance, may also be called attachment, longing, or what Pema Chödrön refers to as "getting hooked." This is a possessive state that wants, clings to, and grasps at objects, both living beings and things.

3. *Anger* is a hostile and aggressive state. Our whole body becomes tight and filled with energy so we can no longer feel ease, comfort, or pleasure. Anger frequently leads to unskillful actions, which lead to even more trouble.

4. *Pride* or arrogance is an inflated feeling of superiority. We do not respect or appreciate others. The teachings say that an arrogant mind is the worst mind to have because it is like an iron ball in the rain: it cannot contain any water. Similarly, a person with an arrogant mind cannot contain spiritual qualities or teachings.

5. *Doubt* or hesitation holds us back because of uncertainty. We may have intentions and aspirations about what we want to do, but as long as we have doubt, we cannot fully accomplish it. If we're not completely sure, why would we care? So then we don't prepare. Doubt holds us back from necessary preparation and necessary action.

6. *Wrong views* are beliefs or opinions influenced by the kleshas. There are five types of erroneous views that are the basis for all other unwholesome views to arise. They are (a) belief in an existent personal self, (b) extremist views such as eternalism and nihilism, (c) not believing in the karmic law of cause and effect, (d) believing that wrong views are the truth, and (e) believing in an erroneous path to liberation.

The six root kleshas can be subsumed into three: ignorance, desire, and anger. Some writers call them confusion, passion, and aggression. Another way of looking at it is that we have three styles of dealing with our inner and outer lives: not noticing (indifference or "ignore-ance," which is confusion), grasping at or pulling toward us (attachment or desire, which is passion), and pushing away from us (aversion, which leads to anger and aggression).

In the very moment when any disturbing emotion arises, we can already see the effect. In the case of anger it is very obvious. If a person is relaxed, smiling, and friendly, and in the next moment suddenly becomes angry, we can immediately see the loss of comfort in the person's facial expression and body language. We can project that into the future and realize: if a disturbing emotion causes discomfort at the very start, how much more distress will there be in the result!

TWENTY SUBSIDIARY KLESHAS

There are twenty disturbing mental or emotional states that are subsidiary to the six root kleshas. Some of them may be translated in different ways when they carry shades of meaning not exactly expressed in the English words. Many of the descriptions that follow are accompanied by specific consequences or effects of these disturbing emotions.

1. *Wrath* or fury is anger that includes violence.

2. *Resentment* is prolonged anger linked to the intention to retaliate in the future. It includes a lack of forgiveness.

3. *Spite* is malice arising from anger and resentment. It causes harsh speech.

4. *Hostility* is a wish to cause harm, marked by lack of affection and sympathy, making a person uncompassionate.

5. *Jealousy* and *envy* are closely related. Jealousy comes from possessiveness and attachment to people and things that we identify as our own possessions. We don't want others to exclusively possess or enjoy what is perceived as "mine." Envy is the inability to bear the excellence or success of others, and the desire to have what others enjoy. Both cause unhappiness and the inability to rest the mind naturally.

6. *Deceit* entails dishonestly concealing one's own faults or mistakes to gain advantage. It results in an attitude of insincerity that blocks the ability to receive spiritual instruction.

7. *Pretense* entails making up self-aggrandizing qualities, motivated by the wish to gain something for oneself. This causes an inability to be genuine.

8. *Lack of conscience* (or lack of embarrassment) leads to the failure to impose limits or restraints on one's behavior.

9. *Shamelessness* means that one does not feel shamed when others object to one's behavior. Both shamelessness and the lack of conscience can lead to nonvirtuous actions.

10. *Concealment* is the inability to do things correctly or properly because we are hiding our mistakes or shortcomings.

11. *Stinginess* is a lack of generosity coming from a strong attachment to material possessions or property, which can make it hard to part with one's possessions.

12. *Self-infatuation* is excessive vanity or excitement about one's own successful qualities.

13. *Lack of interest* implies no appreciation of or interest in virtue and the causes of virtue.

14. *Laziness* or inertia is a failure of diligence that comes from a lack of courage, appreciation for virtuous activities, and exertion. Laziness decreases our abilities, diminishes our qualities, and prevents us from engaging in virtuous actions.

15. *Heedlessness* is a failure to be mindful, careful, or cautious about which actions are virtuous or nonvirtuous. It can strengthen unskillfulness.

16. *Forgetfulness* is the failure to remember the purposes of our good aims or goals. It causes mental distraction and loss of mindfulness.

17. *Non-alertness* is the distraction of discriminating knowledge that occurs with the kleshas. This can lead to careless or inappropriate actions and forgetting previous intentions or vows.

18. *Lethargy* or dullness is a foggy mental state accompanied by a sense of mental or physical heaviness, which can cause a feeling that one cannot meet the challenges of life.

19. *Excitement* is focusing on an object in a desirous way that draws and captures our attention and makes us restless.

20. *Distraction* is the result of a wandering mind that is lost and

cannot rest or remain on the object of focus. It causes an inability to remain one-pointed.

Like a great psychiatrist, the Buddha saw that for most of us, it is the *mental* causes of trouble and suffering that bring the most harm, not external events or conditions. Pragmatically, the Buddha recommended that to attain peace we must decrease all these disturbing mental states, the six root kleshas and twenty subsidiary kleshas, and cultivate skillful, virtuous states.

Skillfulness Checklist

√ Have faith and intelligent trust.
√ Be conscientious, acting with mindful caution.
√ Become pliant, or flexible in mind and body.
√ Practice equanimity, with the mind naturally at rest.
√ Let embarrassment keep you from acting unskillfully.
√ Have healthy shame and do not violate community standards.
√ Practice nonattachment to people and things.
√ Give up hatred and aversion. Don't be upset by anything.
√ Be free from delusion. Investigate carefully.
√ Practice nonviolence out of compassion.
√ Be diligent. Make a joyful effort to do positive things.

The Fifth Skandha: Multiplicity of Consciousness

Mahayana Buddhism analyzes consciousness into eight types of perceiving consciousness: (1–5) five sense-consciousnesses, (6) mental consciousness (mind), (7) klesha consciousness, and (8) storehouse consciousness. In English it is not usual to see the word "consciousnesses" in the plural, as people think of consciousness as being a single thing. But, as we have seen in the teaching on multiplicity, everything can be broken down into smaller components; thus in this context we often speak of "consciousnesses" in the plural, since different types of consciousness can be discerned.

The perceiving consciousnesses originate in six fields, beginning with the five sensory fields of seeing, hearing, smelling, tasting, and touch, and concluding with the field of mental perception or the mental objects that are perceived. The five sense-consciousnesses are nonconceptual or experiential, while the sixth consciousness—the mind, or mental consciousness—is mainly conceptual.

When we meditate, we are using the sixth consciousness, mind. It is this sixth consciousness that becomes familiar with the Four Seals of the Dharma as we meditate on them. Not only does this consciousness come into play when you meditate, but the ten neutral mental factors, particularly focused concentration, are also present.

Another example is when we are learning to practice meditation with a focal point—that is, focusing attention on an object, as when we visualize an image of Shakyamuni Buddha. We use our perceiving consciousnesses to look directly at the entire image for a few minutes. This is using the eyes and eye-consciousness. Then we close our eyes. The mental image that remains is being held in our sixth consciousness, mind. By doing this exercise again and again, we become very familiar with the object of our focus. We can easily recall and visualize the details mentally.

This mental consciousness has a conceptual and a nonconceptual aspect. When we begin to work with Contemplative Meditation, we emphasize the conceptual or analytical mind as a way to understand impermanence, multiplicity, suffering, and emptiness. At the same time, through our conceptual meditation, we are also strengthening the experiential or nonconceptual mind. When the conceptual mind begins to understand the fourth seal, emptiness, by contemplating it again and again, then the conceptual mind begins to become less separated from the object it is contemplating (emptiness).

There comes a time when the union of subject and object occurs. Conceptual mind transforms into nonconceptual mind. It is at this point in the meditation that you, the contemplator, should drop all thoughts and mentally rest quietly for as long as the experience lasts.

The klesha consciousness is inwardly focused and has as its object the storehouse consciousness. In ordinary human beings this klesha consciousness is the "I, me, mine" part, the mind afflicted with ego-clinging. The neutral level called the storehouse consciousness, which is not too clear but aware, serves as the place for storing the seeds or imprints of our karmic actions. This storehouse consciousness is the repository of all our habitual patterns and karmic impressions of past actions.

Imagine that the storehouse consciousness is a great ocean. The waves rising out of the ocean are the five sense-consciousnesses, the mental consciousness, and the klesha consciousness. Just as ocean waves continually rise up and disappear back into the ocean, it is out of the storehouse—often called the "ground" consciousness—that the other seven types of consciousness arise and subside.

Although mind cannot be directly measured by technology, we can measure the results of the mind's functioning through these types of brain chemical changes that occur with the expression of emotional states. Take anger, for example. We can see when someone is angry because the face, body movements, and voice undergo changes. We are not seeing "anger" itself but the external bodily effects that occur as a result of anger.

Buddhism teaches the doctrine of rebirth. This means that our mind, or stream of experience, is a continuum, with past, present, and future lives. The brain is part of the physical form, which ends along with the rest of the body at death, while the stream of experience continues.

Many physicists and doctors accept the idea that consciousness is nonlocal and can't be confined to a place or organ such as the physical brain. A neurosurgeon, Dr. Eban Alexander, reported a near-death experience in which he entered a heavenly realm while in a week-long coma due to meningitis. The fact that he could experience a journey into another world, even though the neurons of his cerebral cortex were completely disabled by the bacterial infection, convinced this man of science that the mind is not dependent on the brain.

The Eight Consciousnesses			
Consciousness	**Sense**	**Object**	**Function**
1. Eye-consciousness	visual	forms	sight
2. Ear-consciousness	auditory	sounds	hearing
3. Nose-consciousness	olfactory	odors	smell
4. Tongue-consciousness	gustatory	flavors	taste
5. Body-consciousness	tactile (skin)	tangible objects	touch
6. Mental consciousness (mind)	mental (brain and nervous system)	phenomena	knowing
7. Klesha consciousness	mental faculty	skandhas	"I"-ness; "I am"; ego-clinging
8. Storehouse consciousness	mental faculty	generalized phenomena	collecting habits, karmic imprints

My Session on Multiplicity

When I do a session of Contemplative Meditation on multiplicity, I begin with form. I think to myself this body has a head, two arms, two legs, and a torso. My body is not one single unit. Looking

In order to gain knowledge about the abiding nature of
   reality,
Know that the five aggregates are not the self
And that the mind believing in the self is not the self, either,
And when you gain certainty in this, rest right within that.

—KHENPO TSULTRIM GYAMTSO, *Stars of Wisdom*

---

around the room, I see many objects, and all of them can be taken
apart.

Feeling is usually started by noticing my present feelings. Is the
strongest feeling a physical sensation like temperature or leg pain,
or is a mental or emotional feeling stronger? I notice how my feelings are continually changing. I ask myself whether they are pleasant, unpleasant, or neutral.

Then, when considering perception, I think about my opinions
and beliefs, which for me are usually on the subject of various reli-
gions, including Buddhism. I notice how many of them I have and
the ways they have changed.

For mental formations, I review the emotional content of the
last fifteen to twenty minutes, remembering as much as possible
what occurred.

The eight perceiving consciousnesses can be explored by planning to have something to taste and smell available during the
session. Let me offer examples from a meditation session. The
thinker of "I want to meditate for twenty minutes" is my mental
consciousness. I see the forest through the large windows in my
meditation room, smell incense, hear the air-conditioner running,
taste a drink of water, and feel my clothes against my skin—that
covers all five sense-consciousnesses. My secretary opens the of-
fice door and the noise interrupts my meditation. The thought,
"Why is she doing this during *my* meditation period?" is the klesha consciousness. For a moment there isn't an object that I am
particularly aware of that would be the storehouse consciousness.

The five skandhas are physical and mental collections, each with many parts that put together make up you and me. Within these collections nothing can be found that is permanent, singular, or unchanging. This is easy to say but hard to internalize, so as contemplators we must first investigate and then contemplate again and again until we achieve certainty that these teachings are true from our own experience. When we reach this point of certainty, we should not stop but continue to strengthen the certainty through repeated sessions of contemplative meditation. As certainty is strengthened, the time spent thinking grows shorter and shorter and the time spent resting in certainty lengthens.

9

The Seal of Suffering

We do things that cause suffering even though we really want peace and happiness.

After the Buddha's enlightenment, he gave his first teachings at the Deer Park in what is now Sarnath, near Varanasi, India. Among these early teachings were the Four Noble Truths:

There is this Noble Truth of suffering: birth is suffering, aging is suffering, sickness is suffering, death is suffering, sorrow and lamentation, pain, grief, and despair are suffering, association with the loathed is suffering, dissociation from the loved is suffering, not to get what one wants is suffering—in short, the five aggregates [skandhas] affected by clinging are suffering.

There is this Noble Truth of the origin of suffering: it is craving, which produces renewal of being, is accompanied by relish and lust, relishing this and that; in other words, craving for sensual desires, craving for being, craving for non-being.

There is this Noble Truth of the cessation of suffering: it is the remainderless fading and ceasing, the giving up, the relinquishing, letting go, and rejecting of that same craving.

There is this Noble Truth of the way leading to the cessation of suffering: it is this Noble Eightfold Path, that is to say: right view, right intention, right speech, right action, right livelihood, right effort, right mindfulness, and right concentration.

—QUOTED IN BHIKKU NYANAMOLI, *Life of the Buddha*

The four main sufferings are described as birth, old age, sickness, and death.

The Woes of Birth and Aging

Traditionally the teachings about suffering actually begin with the situation *before* birth, while we are still in our mother's womb. This is a new idea for most of my Western students, but when you think about it, you may find that it makes sense.

At the moment of conception, when the egg and sperm meet, the process begins whereby the cells gradually grow into an embryo. Although scientists have not yet determined exactly when a fetus experiences pain, it is agreed by many people that in the later months of pregnancy the fetus is sensitive to sounds, maternal emotions, and other impressions. Not all of these are pleasant, even though mothers try to create the best possible environment. The fetus has to undergo uncontrollable changes when the mother moves about, eats different foods, or uses medications or alcohol. The intrauterine state ends abruptly with the compulsory expulsion into this world which we call birth. From then on, although the baby is growing and developing, at the same time he or she is on the track moving inevitably toward aging and death.

In the West the natural aging process is resisted and feared. People try to delay or conceal the signs of age with diets, makeup, hair dye, or medical procedures. Being youthful and desirable into advanced age is considered a great achievement. Yet old age unavoidably brings with it suffering and sadness from the loss of youthful powers, deteriorating health, the death of friends, and being ignored or ridiculed by younger people.

By contrast, elders in Asian countries were traditionally respected, and people used old age as a time to devote themselves to cultivating wisdom. In Tibet, people never even celebrated birthday parties until modern times, and then only in the larger cities. In the area where the yak herders live, birthdays are not yet part of the culture. Soon the idea of birthday parties will arrive and with it the worries about remembering, forgetting, picking out the right present or enough presents, and party planning. For the receiver there are the insecurities of being liked or not liked, judged by the amount and quality of birthday greetings and presents.

I'm not saying birthday parties and presents are bad, because they can be a source of happiness and love, especially for children. But it seems to me that in the West, birthdays and holidays are not always events that people look forward to or activities that bring happiness. Although it may seem like a trivial example of suffering, the stress around birthdays reveals the underlying insecurity, self-doubt, and craving for approval that are sources of much suffering that we create for ourselves.

Traditionally the true beginning of your current lifetime is considered to be at conception, about nine months before your birthday. This date is usually not celebrated or even known exactly. The anniversary of your "conception day" does not make you suffer, does it? Yet through concepts and habitual patterns, we have created the idea of a special day, made it important, and thus initiated the cause of trouble and anxiety for ourselves and others. It can be helpful to remember that the whole custom of parties and presents is fabricated, and this becomes a way we make suffering. Presents or no presents, it's okay, since we were not born with presents.

Holidays, along with family reunions, are also stressful for most people—times that are supposed to make us happy. Most often, the trouble is mental. It can be very intense and begin days and even weeks before the actual holiday or visit. Hope and fear are usually at the root of the problem. These two nasty traps that cause us to expend our mental energy building imaginary situations of this or that happening, being said or done, offered or not offered, and so on. If we could dissolve these mental and emotional sources of suffering, then we might find that, as in the Zen saying, "Every day is a good day."

One way to prevent mental suffering is to observe ourselves and figure out what triggers our problem. If we can identify what makes our blood pressure rise and causes us to feel upset, then we have taken a big step toward seeing the larger picture. With this wider perspective, there is less chance that we will jump back into an old habitual pattern that only makes us feel bad.

It is not that we have to stop going to all family holidays, but that we figure out ways to enjoy the parts that are enjoyable, like the delicious food and the chance to connect with people, and to feel more neutral and detached about the annoying or hurtful moments. We often place too many expectations and requirements on ourselves and those around us. We could give the situation a little space and see what develops. The kindest thing we can do in these situations is to remain calm and refrain from causing more difficulty.

At our meditation center in Memphis, called Pema Karpo ("White Lotus" in Tibetan), I have noticed that after holidays our services are filled with more than the usual number of people. It seems they all need meditation time to recover! I joke to the students that many lotuses, even in the winter, blossom on Pema Karpo's cushions after these stressful holidays.

Mental Suffering

As discussed in the chapter on multiplicity, most mental troubles are due to the six root kleshas. Here I would like to comment on two subjects that are sometimes of concern to Westerners: low self-esteem and suicidal feelings.

The Problem of Low Self-Esteem

Low self-esteem is a well-documented epidemic in the West. Those who suffer from it see themselves and their bodies in distorted ways. I have been told by people who feel this way that they really believe that everyone else feels the same way about them. But it is not so.

Negative qualities and habitual patterns that cause suffering may be hard to see, but also our positive qualities are often hard to see. Scientists say that our brain is designed to notice what is wrong so that we can correct the problem. But this also means that we unrealistically place more emphasis on the negative. If the weather is too hot or cold, everyone complains, but if the temperature is just right, you forget about it and just enjoy yourself. To relax, we need to know ourselves and come to a place of acceptance. This will make life better. Do not be afraid of coming to know yourself very well. No doubt there are some societal patterns that lead to a fear of looking carefully, such as being conditioned to feel guilty over mistakes or sins. A highly competitive school and job system makes people anxious about performance, and the consumer culture bombards us with ads aimed at making everyone believe that they really need and want more and more things.

Competition and comparison are a frequent source of worry and depression. You may fear that you can't meet the requirements that you think are demanded of you, or that you won't do as well as others. Maybe you feel you did not meet your parents' expectations, or you compare yourself negatively to your siblings. You may be out of work, or think that your job is not sufficiently prestigious, your salary not high enough.

Behind these constant anxieties, a primary cause of low self-worth is traumatic experiences and negative messages received in childhood. Negative messages may come in the form of actual child abuse or in more subtle behaviors that make young children feel unloved and unworthy. The problem is made worse because children blame themselves, believing that because they were mistreated, it means that they are fundamentally bad. As an adult, you may need to courageously face the fact that you did not grow up in an ideal environment—and at the same time you must let go of the false idea that this means you are worthless. Even though karmic causes produce whatever bad experiences come to us in life, that is not a reason to condemn ourselves.

People tend to repeat the behaviors they have learned or the treatment they have been subjected to. This is how the habitual patterns of an individual, family, or society develop. Generation after generation, such patterns become stronger and stronger. The wisdom lineages of Buddhist societies produce patterns that are supportive, lessen confusion, and are more reflective of actual reality. They offer a transmission of kindness, compassion, and wisdom. If you uphold these patterns that lead to a good society and good individuals, then you are a wisdom holder. On the other hand, many people become "bad-habitual-pattern lineage holders." We must replace those patterns that we do not want to transmit to the next generation. This requires attentiveness and making mindful effort in daily life.

So the anxious feeling that I am going to find a bad thing if I look deeply at myself is a big stumbling block. If we gather the courage to begin looking at ourselves honestly, then yes, we will see patterns that are not beneficial, but we will also see many that are beneficial. So perhaps "self-esteem" is not the best term. We are not seeking to "esteem" ourselves in the sense of increasing our egoism. A famous line from Shantideva says, "Self-cherishing is the root of all suffering." To be free from suffering, we need to know our true self-*worth*, the value and importance of being the human being that we are, with all the potential that holds.

Most important, we possess buddha-nature, which is the seed of buddhahood—what Chögyam Trungpa Rinpoche called "basic goodness"—which cannot be taken away from us. This means that there are many innate good qualities that we should recognize in ourselves and build upon, for a happier life. As ordinary people our basic goodness is covered over by the two obscurations, emotional and cognitive, so we don't see it or experience it. Contemplation and analysis are ways to remove these obscurations. When all obscurations are completely removed, then buddhahood naturally manifests, and this is called nirvana in Mahayana Buddhism. It is the complete peace and pure happiness (or "great bliss") of full enlightenment. One who is familiar with this has a soft mind, in which few disturbing emotions arise, and when they do arise, they do not stay long but quickly dissolve. Body actions and speech are not aggressive. The person is calmer and has a natural joy.

Dissolving patterns of low self-worth is one of the aims of Contemplative Meditation. This occurs through the confidence gained by knowing ourselves by means of meditative analysis. It is very helpful to look carefully and gently, without pushing, at our own habitual patterns as we study and consider teachings. It is not enough to just read or listen to the teachings. We must contemplate them. We have to work hard, turning the wheel of contemplative analysis again and again. Then, based on clear reasoning, we will be able to see the errors in our thought patterns and to change them.

In the beginning, it can also be helpful to listen carefully to our friends' descriptions of us, since they are seeing us more clearly. It is true they can also see our negative qualities and unhelpful patterns more clearly, too. Yet we also project many views and ideas onto ourselves and onto others. We look at others and think they are better off than we are. Most likely, others are looking at us and thinking the same thing! In fact, people are often looking at us and seeing better qualities.

I attended a conference of Dharma teachers where this subject of self-worth came up in a small discussion group. One teacher asked me, "Why do you think so many Westerners carry darkness within them, a feeling of self-dislike?" I turned the question around by asking why most Tibetans carry a sense of self-worth and feel good about themselves. For the average Tibetan yak herder, a sunny sky, a full stomach, and being alive is enough to make them happy. From birth, Tibetan Buddhists have only heard that they have a precious human birth and buddha-nature. A human birth is not easy to attain and requires mountains of good merit and virtuous works in previous lives. Having it now is itself a cause for celebration and great appreciation. Anyone raised in Tibetan culture has heard these ideas thousands of times.

I have several American students who tell me they hate themselves. They are always worrying about how to change and better themselves because they are not good enough or dissatisfied with how they are at present. This culture tells us we can always do better and be better if we just push a little harder. Why not relax and accept ourselves first? If we do this, we are already a "better" self.

Suicide: The Wrong Way to End Suffering

The news and statistics in the United States are filled with incidents of suicide, and tragically these occur especially among young people who are targets of bullying and our military troops who have been traumatized by war. Although there are treatable causes of suicidal impulses, such as serious depression and post-traumatic stress, as students of the Dharma we should understand that killing yourself is the worst possible choice you can make, under the mistaken belief that it means escaping from suffering. Suicide is like giving a beautiful house away in favor of living in a very bad place. From a Buddhist perspective, it means losing a rare chance to free oneself from suffering, because a human birth is hard to attain.

Since childhood I have been trained that to be born human is the best possible outcome among the six possible realms of rebirth in samsara. Compared with animals, there are advantages to our makeup that we tend to take for granted. Our brains are very well developed. We are intelligent and are able to communicate. We have memory and the ability to visualize well. Having developed writing and reading, we are able to save and to pass on our knowledge. Science has shown that certain other animals display communication, self-awareness, empathy, tool making, and other human-like traits. But although a dog may make the news because he can skateboard, even the smartest dog on the planet cannot make a skateboard. According to the Dharma, all beings possess the buddha-nature, the seed of enlightenment, but only in the human form can we consciously realize that nature and become fully enlightened.

Several students have confided to me that they had thoughts of suicide. This is not the way to end suffering. From the Buddhist point of view, suicide is a direct cause of a great deal more trouble and suffering. Not only will your family and friends be devastated, but you will have killed the most important human being in your life—the one who has the power to benefit yourself and others in many wonderful ways. Suicide is the clearest example of wishing to end suffering while in fact causing much, much more.

One friend of mine shared with me over many tasty meals how he became a Buddhist. It began with a girlfriend who tried to get close to him. Because of his past, this was very difficult for him. He could not relax and allow a more intimate relationship to develop. Over time he realized that this was no good, and so he began to try to develop a closer relationship with her. But because of past patterns he did this in an anxious and grasping way that turned her away from him.

One day she told him that he was not the one she wanted as a partner. She wanted to have children and he did not. She had found another person and was leaving him.

On the outside he appeared to be a very strong person, but inside he was very afraid and lonely. During the day he taught school but at night would come home alone feeling bad and that his life was falling apart. He would pick up the phone to call someone and hang up before dialing.

One day he realized he needed to do something good for himself. He bought a cookbook, set a beautiful table, and prepared a

Even though you wish to abandon suffering,
You continue to chase after its cause.
Even though you desire happiness,
Out of delusion you treat your happiness as an enemy.

—SHANTIDEVA, *Bodhicharyavatara*

---

nice meal for himself. He served himself very beautifully, ate, and felt better. Next he purchased a Dharma book and read it over and over again. Gradually he became a dedicated practitioner—and a great cook. I have enjoyed his company and cooking many times over the years.

We must learn to observe our situation and figure out ways to change the patterns that cause us to suffer. My heart advice is to do good things that benefit yourself and others in the present moment. Many present moments equal the future, which becomes the present and then the past. If we do meritorious actions in the present moment, then we will continue doing good for our whole life.

Sickness and Pain

Sickness is part of life. When you find yourself confronting illness in your own or others' lives, it is important to be open and let go of your clinging to the belief that sickness and pain are solid, stable realities. Like everything else, they are impermanent and made of multiple changing parts.

If a physical problem cannot be treated or cured, then accepting and not resisting what can't be changed sometimes unexpectedly brings improvement to the condition. I think meditation helps sickness. I often say to students that meditation is not only food for the mind; it is medicine too. Mind and body are not the same, but they work together. When the mind relaxes and rests in the meditative state, the body receives positive energy. I myself have been helped by using meditation when I get headaches. Therapies have been developed that apply meditation as a way to deal with chronic pain with specific techniques. For example, instead of fixing attention on the pain, or trying to distract attention away from the pain, you learn to observe the sensations neutrally and notice how the pain is not continuous as you thought, but is actually broken up into segments, and you can rest your mind in the intervals. This is just one example of a way to relate with suffering through understanding the truths of multiplicity and impermanence.

Too much talking about suffering is not helpful, but this way of talking about transforming it is.

Inspiration may also be found in the example of great masters, such as Gyalse Ngulchu Thogme, the fourteenth-century author of works such as *The Thirty-seven Verses on the Practice of a Bodhisattva*. His Holiness Dilgo Khyentse Rinpoche has written about how, when Gyalse Thogme became sick, someone asked him if there was any way to prolong his life. Thogme replied, "If my being sick will benefit beings, may I be blessed with sickness! If my dying will benefit beings, may I be blessed with death! If my being well will benefit beings, may I be blessed with recovery! This is the prayer I make to the Three Jewels. Having complete certainty that whatever happens is the blessing of the Three Jewels, I am happy, and I shall take whatever happens onto the path without trying to change anything."

When Death Comes

Fear of death is common in the West, even though popular culture celebrates death-defying sports and violent entertainments. Even autopsies, real or fictional, are shown on television, yet people don't like to talk about death. Americans who hear a little about Buddhism may form the impression that we put too much emphasis on death, always reminding ourselves that we can be snatched away at any time. But it is not because we are morbid or pessimistic that Buddhists remember death. It is to keep us focused on what really matters, our spiritual values and priorities.

When death comes, the mind separates from the body and goes wherever our mental habit patterns take us. For most of us, that means rebirth in one of the six realms of samsara. Remembering how quickly life passes and the inevitability of death can inspire us to practice and make efforts while there is still time, for no one knows when their time will come. The understanding that this life is not the only one and that our stream of experience will take birth again motivates us to stay on the path of merit, because positive thoughts and actions will result in a happy, fortunate rebirth, while negative thoughts and actions lead to suffering.

A main reason people find it difficult to accept death is the fear of letting go of their attachment to loved ones, possessions, and experiences, as well as clinging to their ego identity. I would like to tell you the story of someone who met death with a positive attitude and view: my father, Dechen Chogyal, who passed away on February 15, 2011. The extended family and friends were fortunate in being able to observe the example that he set. We, too, were able to accept his death without attachment, despite our sadness at losing him.

My older sister, a nun in lifelong retreat, said at the time, "Now is the right time for him to go and he is ready. It is proper that old parents are able to die ahead of their children. When the children die first and the parents are old, they are left with great suffering in their old age." Even my mother was not upset or crying when it became clear that my father was dying, but continued practicing and reciting mantras with faith.

Dechen Chogyal first became very ill while on retreat with my mother and sister in December 2010. Because he felt he was near the end, he moved from the retreat place to the family's yak herder's hut high in the mountains and began to prepare himself according to our tradition. Our family has been practitioners of the Nyingma lineage for many generations, and he had total confidence in the Dharma.

He told his eldest son that he wished the family to arrange to have three sutras carved into stone for him. A monastery was contacted and asked to carve these sutras and place the stones at a very special place blessed by the great master Patrul Rinpoche.

Then my father began the traditional devotional practice of molding and firing small statues called *tsa-tsas,* made from local pottery clay. Normally he slept a great deal or rested in his bed, saying mantras and turning his prayer wheel. Now he would awaken at five and make the small statues all day long. While making them, he would tell neighbors and visitors in a joking, light-hearted way that he was going to die soon.

At the request of other family members, he was moved to the home of his eldest son with the hope that he would seek medical care. However, he told us, "No, no, I don't want to go to the hospital. I am seeing a local doctor and I am taking his medicine. If this medicine helps, then it will lengthen my life; if it doesn't, then my life will end." When the doctor came, he brought three days' worth of medicine. My father concluded, "Now I have three days of life left."

The last time we spoke, on the phone, was a wonderful conversation. He told me: "Everything I wished for has been accomplished. I was able to go on pilgrimage to all the sacred places. At each place I prayed and dedicated the merit for all sentient beings. I was not only thinking of myself but of all beings. Now I don't have any problems. I have no regrets." I thought, "Well, he is okay." Although I was a little bit sad, it was bearable. I knew that he was relaxed and present, and that this was a good way to die.

The day before my father died, he was still very strong, relaxed, and able to speak. He wasn't nervous, afraid, or in pain. When visitors came, he gave them advice and Dharma teachings. He told them, "Look at your situation carefully and do what you need to do to keep your family and yourself alive. When you die, you cannot take anything with you except what you have learned of the Dharma and your good heart and mind."

He said, "It is very important to always dedicate the virtue to all sentient beings. You should not do any non-virtuous activities, not even a little, such as actions that disturb other people's minds. It is very important always to have a good heart." He repeated, "I have no attachments and no regret. Don't worry about me." Right up to the end, he was concerned with the welfare of others and giving them his heart advice.

Then, slowly, as the process of dying continued, he became unable to talk anymore. He was still present and relaxed. The family saw that his mind was clear. When visitors would come, he would touch his heart and join his palms in the gesture of prayer as he silently offered his final words of advice.

When his grandson, who is a monk, was at his bedside reading aloud from the *Bardo Thodrol* (Liberation through Hearing in the Bardo)—the classic text of instructions for the after-death period—it was clear that he understood what was being read to him. His breath became shorter and shorter, until it stopped. The family described it as being like a butter lamp going out when the last of the fuel is gone.

My father was a simple yak herder, devoted to the Dharma. He did not know how to read, but he could recite many mantras and was always doing dedications of merit and aspirations that all sentient beings would be liberated, have no suffering, and be happy. He was a very good-hearted person. My sister told me once about the time they saw some little baby goats that were abandoned because their mother had died. She said he was so touched that he cried, and she saw clearly his kind heart and his compassion.

Dechen Chogyal had spent many years in a Chinese prison in the early 1960s. At that time, he received very good teachings from great lamas who were imprisoned along with him. Many times he repeated the heart instruction they had given: that the very bad situation in Tibet was not just the fault of the Chinese and that our negative karma was being dissolved. They said, "We should not feel anger or hatred and act badly toward the Chinese. Instead, we need to raise compassion and dedicate all our virtue to them first."

Those who practice from the heart, even uneducated persons like my father, have true power.

Three Types of Suffering

Suffering is divided into three main categories. The first two categories are well known by us all. The third is a more subtle, pervasive problem.

1. *The suffering of suffering* is like the series of calamities that Job suffered in the Old Testament. Or, as Patrul Rinpoche described it in *Words of My Perfect Teacher,* "We get leprosy, and then we break out in boils, too; and then as well as breaking out in boils, we get injured." In a modern example, people who survive a violent hurricane may suffer not only the death or injury of family members but also the destruction of their homes and possessions and the loss of pets— suffering upon suffering.

This category includes the sufferings of birth, aging, sickness, and death, as well as not getting what you want, having to deal with what you don't want, and the loss of what you love. It also includes the terrible sufferings of the three non-human lower realms: the beings of the hot and cold hells, the hungry ghosts, and the animal realm.

2. *The suffering of change* includes every uncomfortable, painful, problematic occurrence that comes about because of change, whether it is a small inconvenience like an unwanted interruption of your plans, or a more dramatic example like a sudden loss or a hurtful disappointment.

3. *All-pervasive suffering* is the most subtle of the three types. Because of impermanence, the fact that everything is always changing in each moment, we can never really satisfy

our desires completely or make the satisfaction last. Thus, life as it is lived in samsara is unsatisfactory by its very nature. This category is subtle because it means that, in a sense, we suffer all the time, often silently and invisibly, not just from obvious causes like the violence of war, crimes, natural disasters, injuries and illnesses, or emotional and mental traumas. We suffer because it seems that life never brings the lasting fulfillment we hope for.

In addition, even the good things that life brings to us unavoidably cause suffering to other beings. Consider elections, and sporting events and contests, in which for every happy winner there is an unhappy loser. Living in the American South, with its barbecued meat specialties, we are often reminded of how human diners enjoy their meals at the expense of pigs, cows, and chickens, not to mention the millions of turkeys who are the centerpiece of the national Thanksgiving meal.

All-pervasive suffering is most painful for beings who are spiritually advanced, while ordinary people may not even be aware of it. The traditional analogy uses the image of a single hair resting on the palm of the hand. To the noble beings called Arya Bodhisattvas, it is as irritating and uncomfortable as if the hair were touching their eyeball. But ordinary people probably would not notice the presence of a small hair on their palm.

10

The Seal of Emptiness

When we awaken to emptiness as the true nature of reality, we will experience nirvana, which is ultimate peace and happiness.

I have taught about emptiness at many Dharma centers in North America. One time, when the talk was followed by questions, a woman asked me if I could use a different word, because "emptiness" gave her a feeling of loss. I lightheartedly suggested that she could be right, since understanding emptiness would require the loss of ego-clinging. To those who haven't studied Mahayana Buddhism, this word might appear senseless, but consider this: if it didn't have great import, why would the Buddha have repeated it hundreds of thousands of times?

Emptiness (*shunyata* in Sanskrit) doesn't mean nothingness. That would be nihilism, an extreme view rejected by Buddhism. The famous paradoxical saying from the Heart Sutra declares that "form is emptiness, emptiness also is form." This means that forms and emptiness are inseparable. In fact, all "appearances" (of which physical form is one part) are inseparable from emptiness. It is important to understand that *the inseparability of emptiness and appearances allows everything we accept as our daily life to occur.* In order for there to be any sort of appearance, we need emptiness,

There is not the slightest difference
Between samsara and nirvana.
There is not the slightest difference
Between nirvana and samsara.

—NAGARJUNA, *Mulamadhyamaka-karika*
(Fundamental Wisdom of the Middle Way)

---

and whenever anything appears, it is empty in nature. All appearances, all phenomena, have this quality of being empty of an unchangeable, singular, true existence. Thanks to emptiness, there is an openness in which all the relative phenomena of samsara can change.

If you look deeply, you will find that your own mind is a great personal example of emptiness. Your mind in its natural state is without form, directions, and attributes. Like the sky or open space, it is vast and free from all limitation.

Ordinarily, you experience many changing states of mind, moods, and imaginings. You may have regrets about things done in the past or worries about possible future events. These thoughts cause great suffering in the present, yet they have no true existence. The root cause of suffering is the strong belief and misperception that a true and permanent self exists. The most powerful antidote to the burden of clinging to our existence, with all its hopes and fears, is to know emptiness.

The wisdom of emptiness dispels our confusion. Those who have attained this wisdom view themselves and the world through the lens of emptiness, in which everything is like a dream or an illusion. Those who do not understand emptiness live in a world of attachment, grasping, dissatisfaction, and suffering.

Emptiness is traditionally taught with two different subjects: "emptiness of self" has the self as its subject, and "emptiness of other" has phenomena as its subject. The Mahayana point of view is that both kinds of emptiness—the emptiness of our individual mind and the emptiness of all phenomena—are one. This is called great emptiness, which is the experience of nonduality.

What Is Selflessness?

"Selflessness," the absence of self, is an important Dharma concept. In the dictionary, "selflessness" is defined as unselfishness, but that is not what we mean here. "Selflessness" is often used as a synonym for "emptiness," because when we say that our true nature is empty, we mean empty of self.

How can we understand being devoid of self? For most people the most important person in the world is "myself." It seems natural to think that this self called "I" exists.

Buddhism does not deny that there is an "I" or "I am"; what we are saying is that it exists interdependently, based on the five skandhas of form, feeling, perception, mental formations, and consciousness. The point of contemplation is to know with certainly that "I," the five skandhas, do not exist in a permanent, unchanging, and independent way.

Thinking that I am the same person in the morning as I am in the evening is an example of the mistaken view of a self that is permanent, unchanging, and independent. The morning and evening person is not completely the same. Yet this is the way we normally think about ourselves and what we cling to as a stable identity. Yet by holding this erroneous view, we suffer and cause suffering. No person, no object or phenomenon in our reality, stays the same as a single entity. This is happening whether we realize it or not, whether we believe it or not. Knowing this truth allows us to be open to, and even expect, the changes and shifts, both positive and negative, that will inevitably occur. It allows us to more easily accept ourselves, our family and friends, our environment.

From a relative point of view, it is valid and reasonable to say that this singular "I" exists. Conventionally we identify and name ourselves, other sentient beings, plants, minerals, and things. When we speak of ourselves, it is natural to use the word "I" or "me." Buddhism agrees that the five skandhas we label "I" do exist conventionally. However, from an ultimate point of view, this "I" does not exist. This ultimate view—selflessness, or emptiness—is found in the prajnaparamita teachings of the Heart Sutra.

What Is Nirvana?

Although we have stated the fourth seal as "Our true nature is emptiness," it is also possible to phrase it as "Nirvana is peace." Nirvana here is equated with emptiness, selflessness (absence of self), ultimate peace, and buddha-nature. Nirvana is a state of perfect happiness, serene and joyful. It is not a temporary happiness that ebbs and flows, but is stable and free from any conceptual or dualistic mind. In this statement we are talking about absolute truth, free from all elaborations and kleshas.

Nirvana is not somewhere else; we do not "go" to nirvana, but when our mental perceptions change—when wisdom grows and confusion lessens—then automatically there is a change in what appears to our perception.

In Hinayana Buddhism, nirvana means the cessation of suffering through not being reborn in the six realms of existence (samsara) and being free from the klesha obscurations, but not completely free from the cognitive obscurations. In contrast, the Mahayana views nirvana as the complete manifestation of our mind's fundamental nature (emptiness). This means the removal of both of the two obscurations—cognitive (the dualistic part) and klesha (emotional). Our fundamental mind is without any disturbing emotions and also without the underlying causes that would cause these disturbing emotions ever to arise again. The Heart Sutra explains the Mahayana nirvana.

Earlier in the book, it was said that when you clearly understand the first three seals—impermanence, multiplicity, and suffering—

then you will automatically know what emptiness means. Repeated analysis and contemplation help you to form a concept of emptiness, to prepare for the experience of emptiness. Chapter 12, "The Four Contemplations," contains some exercises for contemplating the seal of emptiness (see pages 152–55). Then, in part five, the line-for-line commentary and practices that follow the Heart Sutra translation offer more detailed comments on the fourth seal.

Emptiness Checklist

√ There is no permanent existence of a real separate "self" independent of others.

√ The fundamental nature of all phenomena and all beings is great emptiness.

√ Emptiness is freedom from all limitations, like the openness of all-encompassing space.

√ Knowledge of emptiness is the antidote to ego-clinging, with all its attachments, grasping, and fear.

√ True experiences of emptiness include the arising of the great warmth of compassion.

√ When we awaken to the true nature of reality as emptiness, we experience the ultimate peace and happiness of nirvana.

Part Four

*Contemplating
the Four Seals*

11

Preparing for Practice

We prepare ourselves for the main contemplations by using supportive thoughts and images that motivate us to practice.

If you want to go for a drive, it takes a lot more than jumping into the car and sitting behind the wheel. You have to know how to drive, and then you have to start the engine, engage the gears, and so on. In the same way, meditation has structure. In this book, you are learning an approach that has been used to great benefit for hundreds of years.

Time and Place

When we conduct a formal session of meditation, we must have a suitable place. This place could be anywhere: our bedroom, a separate meditation room, or at a meditation center. What is most important is that the place is quiet and we will not be disturbed or feel uncomfortable while we are there. It is important to feel safe and relaxed.

The seat may be a cushion, a chair, a couch, or a bed, but it needs to be a comfortable seat. Because we have a strong habitual pattern of falling asleep whenever we are lying down, it is recommended to sit upright.

After setting up your meditation space, you need to stay there for a time. In the beginning, when you are establishing your practice patterns, deciding on a time and sticking to it is more important than the actual length of the session. You can negotiate with yourself, saying, "For those five or ten minutes I will stay focused and deal with the rest later."

If you say, "Okay, I'll sit down for ten minutes," and after two minutes you remember, "Oh, I need to do something," or if the phone rings and you jump up, that will create a problem because you will have that imprint in your mind. Instead of learning how to stay focused and how to rest, you are training in just the opposite.

Ideally, aim toward a period of at least twenty-five minutes to thoroughly contemplate each one of the four topics. In the beginning, while learning the formal practice, you probably won't have time to finish every step. But once you become familiar with the practice, the beginning and closing steps will take only a few minutes, and the four contemplations will form the major part of the session. A complete session would thus take about one hour in all.

It's okay to work your way gradually toward a complete session. So, for example, you could start by giving anywhere from five to fifteen minutes to each seal. Or you might contemplate just one seal at your first session, move on to the next seal in the next day's practice, and so on. The more you practice, the easier it will be for you to think about each seal in a way that brings you to the feeling of certainty.

When the opportunity arises to meditate for a long period, your mind will start out fresh and focused, but as you continue, it naturally tends to get weaker and weaker. I find it helpful to fully engage in the Contemplative Meditation practice for a short period of time and then, without leaving my seat, pause for a minute to refresh, and then resume practice.

The first thing I do when I take my seat to meditate is arouse some energy and joy, and thankfulness that I have the time and ability to meditate. Then I take the best meditation posture I can, being sure my spine is upright and my head is balanced properly on my neck and shoulders. I vary between the two main placements of the hands, which are resting in the lap or on the thighs. Sometimes, if I feel sleepy or dull, I sit with my eyes open; at other times, when I've been preoccupied or my surroundings are busy, I sit with my eyes closed. When I feel my posture is correct, I take several deep, slow breaths, relaxing more and more with each out-breath. This moves me naturally into the meditation session.

Meditation Posture and Breathing
Seven Points of Posture

The best meditation posture is called the Seven-Point Posture of Vairochana. Although this posture is recommended, I want to make it clear that we should each find our own way to sit comfortably. Having an upright posture with the spine straight is more important than folding your legs in an unfamiliar or difficult way. Also, although sitting on a cushion on the floor is traditional, some people need to be seated on a chair. You can try to approximate the recommended posture and, having done so, relax and be satisfied with the posture that works for you. Even for me, sitting with my legs fully crossed on my thighs for a long period is very difficult. Here, the saying "Not too tight, not too loose" is important to remember.

The Seven-Point Posture of Vairochana

1. You are seated with your legs crossed in the vajra position, with feet resting on the thighs (full lotus pose), soles turned upward.
2. Your hands either rest palms up in your lap, with the right hand over the left, thumbs touching, or rest palms down on the thighs.

3. Sit up straight. Your spine should be in perfect alignment as much as possible.

4. Your head should be balanced at the top of the spine. Point your chin downward so that it just barely presses down on the front of your neck, where the larynx protrudes.

5. Your shoulders are relaxed and held back slightly, so that the chest is open.

6. Allow your jaws to be relaxed so that the mouth is slightly open. The tip of the tongue should lightly touch the upper palate just behind the top front teeth.

7. Your gaze is gentle, unmoving, and directed toward the tip of your nose, or downward and out about a distance of six feet. You could also gaze right into open space, or settle the gaze somewhere in that in-between space. See what works best for you.

Breathing

After assuming the meditation posture, we do a simple practice, called the Ninefold Exhalation, to clear the stale air from our lungs.

The Ninefold Exhalation

The Ninefold Exhalation is a deep-breathing exercise to remove any stale air from the lungs and replace it with fresh air. It is helpful upon awakening in the morning or anytime you find yourself tense and holding your breath. Here we are using it to begin the session of Contemplative Meditation.

Begin each breath by making a deep inhalation in a way that is comfortable for you.

1. *First breath.* Close the right nostril with your right index finger. Exhale through the left nostril in three parts. The first two parts are short, and then at the end of the exha-

lation an extra push is given so that all the air leaves your lungs.

2. *Second breath*. Close the left nostril with your left index finger, and breathe out through the right nostril, exhaling in the same way as for breath 1. Be sure to conclude with an extra push at the end of the exhalation.

3. *Third breath*. Place your palms on your thighs, and do the threefold exhalation once more, this time through both nostrils.

After completing the Ninefold Exhalation, begin a gentle, relaxed, natural rhythm of breathing. Use whichever one of these three methods is comfortable for you:

- Breathe through both nostrils;
- Breathe through the slightly opened mouth, with the tip of the tongue lightly touching the upper palate, just behind the top front teeth; or
- Breathe through both the nostrils and the mouth.

I find it helpful to regularly breathe in gently and deeply with the mouth closed and then breathe out gently and completely through the mouth and nose while relaxing the body. This breathing technique can be done several times during a practice session. It can also be used in daily life to relax and oxygenate the body and relieve stress and worry.

Your erect body posture will ensure that the inner energy channels are straight. When the inner channels are straight, then the breath can flow smoothly, without obstacles, through all the paths of the body. Smooth breathing in turn ensures a smooth mind, as our breathing process is closely related to our mental state and awareness.

Sometimes there is a feeling of congestion in the chest around the heart. It feels as if all the movement of breathing is in the upper part

Not Too Tight and Not Too Loose

There is a story regarding the Buddha which recounts how he once gave teaching to a famous sitar player who wanted to study meditation. The musician asked, "Should I control my mind or should I completely let go?" The Buddha answered, "Since you are a great musician, tell me how you would tune the strings of your instrument." The musician said, "I would make them not too tight and not too loose." "Likewise," said the Buddha, "in your meditation practice you should not impose anything too forcefully on your mind, nor should you let it wander." That is the teaching of letting the mind *be* in a very open way, of feeling the flow of energy without trying to subdue it and without letting it get out of control, of going with the energy pattern of the mind. This is meditation practice.

—CHÖGYAM TRUNGPA, *Cutting Through Spiritual Materialism*

---

of the body, and the breath seems to be stuck there. At the same time you may feel irritated, anxious, or agitated. There may be tension in the muscles in the neck. All these are signs that the inner breathing process is stuck and blocked in this part of the body. This blockage greatly affects your mental and emotional states. Knowing this, you can make sure that your breathing is very deep, gentle, and smooth. First take a deep, gentle in-breath and then breathe out, allowing any stress and tension to relax and flow from your body, especially the shoulders, neck, and upper chest. This will help make your flow of awareness likewise gentle and smooth.

Posture and Breathing Checklist

√ Your body is seated upright with a straight spine.

√ Your head is slightly bent, balanced on the top of the neck.

√ Your hands rest in the lap or on the thighs.

√ Your chest is open.

√ Your gaze is relaxed.

√ Your breath is smooth.

√ Both your posture and your attention are "not too tight and not too loose."

12

The Four Contemplations

"When we are meditating, we are discovering our mind."
—SAKYONG MIPHAM RINPOCHE

Paradoxically, actual Contemplative Meditation begins almost at the conclusion of the session, when you reach a mental state of certainty about the four subjects: impermanence, multiplicity, suffering, and emptiness. But to arrive at this state of certainty requires thinking and reflecting on each subject. We therefore begin with contemplating the subject until we have no doubt of the truth. At that point we stop thinking about it and sit quietly with the certainty as long as possible. You might say we are meditating on this certainty. Texts sometimes speak of meditating on, or with, "the view," and this is what they mean.

Each time you begin a session of Contemplative Meditation, return to thinking or considering the subject matter until that mental state of certainty is again experienced. By repeating the contemplations again and again, you will become familiar with this mental state of certainty. Then you'll be able to stay in this state, doing Contemplative Meditation for longer periods of time.

In a session you can consider a variety of subjects that are within the main topic. It is useful to use your own habitual patterns, concepts, opinions, and emotions as the basis for your contemplation. It will be helpful to make the contemplative sessions personal, realistic, and relevant to your own experiences.

We have said that we would use the five skandhas as an analytical tool, by breaking down the object of contemplation into the five groups: form, feeling, perception, mental formations, and consciousness (see chapter 8). If you wish, in order to simplify the meditation, you may condense the five skandhas into three general parts: forms, mental formations, and consciousness. Mental formations include feelings and perceptions: the perceptual function recognizes the features of an object that we sense (its shape, color, etc.) and discriminates one thing from another. Feeling occurs when the senses make contact with various objects and any of three kinds of sensations may arise (pleasant, unpleasant, or neutral). The reason why feeling and perception are listed separately, even though they are also included among the mental formations, is that some human beings tend to react based on feelings, both emotional and sensory, while others tend to react based on their philosophical view or set of tenets.

For each contemplation of one of the Four Seals, remember to begin with the preliminary steps as instructed in part two, and to dedicate the merit at the close of each session.

STEPS OF CONTEMPLATIVE MEDITATION

Posture and Breathing

- Sit comfortably in meditation posture on a cushion or chair.
- Bring your awareness into the present moment by becoming aware of your physical body.
- Expel stale air using the Ninefold Exhalation. (See pages 136–37.)
- Sit as still as possible. Breathe deeply and smoothly.

Preliminary Steps

- Arouse the intention to exert yourself by appreciating the body and life that allow you to practice. (See chapter 3.)
- Visualize the Buddha as a figure of wisdom light. (See chapter 4.)
- Recall, in order, the steps of the Seven-Branch Offering. (See chapter 5.)
  1. Appreciating
  2. Offering
  3. Taking responsibility for mistakes
  4. Rejoicing in the goodness of others
  5. Requesting the teachings
  6. Asking the teachers to remain and teach
  7. Dedicating the merit to all beings
- Arouse bodhichitta. (See chapter 6.)

The Meditation

- Contemplate, in order, the Four Seals of the Dharma, giving each equal time.
  Impermanence
  Multiplicity
  Suffering
  Emptiness
- Dedicate the merit for the benefit of all beings.

Contemplation of Impermanence

What does impermanence mean? What are some examples of impermanence in your life? What is the benefit of contemplating impermanence? These are some of the questions you can address in the session on impermanence. (Review chapter 7 if necessary.) Any subject matter that helps you comprehend the understanding that your moment-to-moment life is ever shifting and changing is a good choice for contemplation. Some possibilities are time, aging, personal life, relationships, history, geography, and the entertainment world. Whatever subject you choose, consider, "How is this an example of impermanence?"

Time is a good example to illustrate the method of investigating impermanence. Reflect back on the ten minutes before you sat down to begin the session. Take some time to recall as much detail as possible. What were your movements? Did you eat or drink anything? Change your clothing? Were you speaking? Thinking about something? Can you remember specific conversations or thoughts? How many changes can you remember, both physical and mental, that have occurred in the previous ten-minute time period?

Contemplation of Multiplicity

In a session on multiplicity, we use the five skandhas to contemplate ourselves or any animate or inanimate thing. Thus, Jamgon Mipham Rinpoche begins his instructions for analytical meditation by saying:

Wherever there is an object of particular attachment,
Envision it clearly in front of your mind
And separate it into the five skandhas.

Any object could be chosen, but as a first example, let us see how we might conduct a session on the body.

If you read Jamgon Mipham Rinpoche's text in the Readings section of part five, you will see that in analyzing the human body, he emphasizes the unpleasant parts such as blood, fat deposits, pus, and mucus. Traditionally, this was the classic way for the monastic meditator to counteract any excessive or inappropriate attachment to a generalized concept of the physical body. When I taught this approach at several of Shambhala International's centers, many of the students said that it made them uncomfortable to think about the body as bad, unclean, or, as Mipham describes in his text, "a pile of manure." In Western culture, the overemphasis on the body's appearance, comfort, and desirability, and the embarrassment that people have about the natural functions of the body, make this reaction understandable. But the intention of this type of Buddhist contemplation is not to make the meditator feel sinful or impure. Our aim is to view the human body in a more objective or neutral way, as it is, in order to relax some of our problematic attachments. Remember that there is a distinction between the *reality* of the body as it is and your feelings (attraction or aversion) or concepts about the body as a unitary entity. As it is, the body is no more than a collection of components made up of the five elements, and when you consider its separate parts one by one, especially the unpleasant insides of the body, you realize that you don't feel any attachment to them. The body is, in fact, empty of any true existence to be attached to. Repeated analysis will convince you that this is so.

Contemplation of the Body

Breathe in deeply with the mouth closed.

Breathe out completely through the mouth and nose while relaxing the body.

Form (physical body). Sit upright on your cushion or chair, and sense your whole body. Become aware of your chest and abdomen . . . your arms and hands . . . your legs and feet . . . and your head. Notice your chest rising and falling with your breath. Sense your heart beating. Be conscious of your other inner organs and the many interior parts of the body.

Feeling. Breathing deeply, continue to relax the body. As the breath flows out, allow the physical tension and tightness to be released. Notice how you feel about your body in this present moment. Is it a pleasant or unpleasant feeling? Or is the feeling indifferent or neutral?

Perception. Continue to breathe deeply and slowly. Take a few minutes to watch your thoughts: the discrimination between objects, your concepts about them, and so on.

Mental formations (thoughts and emotions, virtuous and nonvirtuous states). Still breathing deeply and slowly, notice whether any emotions have arisen so far during the session. Has any emotional state changed since the session started? Quietly and as nonjudgmentally as possible, think about any recent or ongoing mental states you can recall and, if possible, give them a name, such as anger, jealousy, or regret. The disturbing emotions are often easier to notice and remember, but also notice positive emotions such as love, compassion, forgiveness, and joy. Review chapter 8, the section "The Fourth Skandha: Multiplicity of Mental Formations," to help identify the virtuous and nonvirtuous mental states and kleshas that are summarized there.

Consciousness. Finally, focus on the sense-consciousnesses and their objects. Look around and notice what the eye-consciousness is seeing. Listen deeply and notice what the ear-consciousness can hear. How is your sense of touch being engaged by the body-consciousness? What do you smell and taste with the nose-consciousness and tongue-consciousness? The sixth consciousness, the mental consciousness or mind, is noticing what all the senses are seeing, hearing, tasting, and so on. The klesha consciousness is what knows that it is "I" who is doing the contemplation. The storehouse consciousness is a general consciousness that does not have a particular focus.

Contemplation of "Myself"

When we analyze our mind in meditation, we find five kinds of experience, but we cannot find any "I" who is having the experience. According to the Buddha Dharma, there is no permanent, unchanging "I" or "self" to be found anywhere. What we call "myself" or "I" is an ever-changing collection of multiple parts. These parts—grouped into five main parts, the skandhas—do not constitute an independent, self-existing entity and therefore are not considered a self that has true existence in its own right.

But we do not see this truth. Because of our illusion that we do have a solid identity, we become attached to the notion of "myself," and this attachment or ego-clinging gives rise to the disturbing mental states called the kleshas. In turn, the result of the kleshas, such as ignorance, anger, pride, jealousy, and other poisons, is suffering of all kinds. Thus, the goal of our contemplation is to discover whether a singular permanent "self" can be found in the skandhas. We think about this thoroughly, until we are certain about it: there is no "myself" in the skandhas. Understanding and internalizing this truth will eliminate a great deal of suffering from our lives.

If the preceding paragraph sounds familiar, it is because it has been stated already in several different ways. It is through a repeated investigation, continually turning the wheel of contemplation, that we come to self-knowledge that is experiential and not just a doctrine that we believe in with blind faith.

As in the "Contemplation of the Body" example (pages 145–46), use the five skandhas to contemplate "myself":

Form. Sense your body as you did in the body contemplation. Now ask yourself: Is this body "myself"? Where in the body can I find "myself"? Am I in my arms or legs? My face or head? My chest? If I lost an arm or a leg, would "I" exist in the detached limb? Does this body belong to "me"? If so, who am I apart from "my" body? Conclusion: My body is a collection of parts, none of which is "myself."

Feeling. Shut your eyes, breathe in and out deeply several times, and bring your attention to the felt sense of your body. As you breathe out, relax your shoulders and feel your body more deeply. Where is "myself" in the felt sense of the body? Is "I" part of the felt sense of the body? Notice the physical and mental feelings that are occurring right now and ask yourself: Where is this "I" who feels? "Who" experiences a feeling to be pleasant, unpleasant, or neutral? Conclusion: There are many different feelings, both physical and mental, within the body, but the "I" cannot be found within feelings.

Perception. Am "I" in my concepts, or in what I believe? What if I changed my belief? Would "I" then become a different me? Are other people's opinions about me part of "me"? Conclusion: "I" cannot be found in beliefs, concepts, and opinions.

Mental formations. Is my name really part of "me," or is it just a conceptual label? Are the emotions that "I" experience part of "me"? Do "I" become a different person if my emotions change—when I get angry or jealous, for example, or when I feel love or compassion? Conclusion: My emotions and the conceptual labels applied to this body or mind are not "myself."

Consciousness. Relax and gently become aware of the objects of your five senses. Look around and listen deeply. Relaxing even more, breathe in and out and notice any smells. Feel your clothes touching your skin, your body resting on the meditation seat, your feet on the floor or resting on your thighs. If you wish, you may have a piece of chocolate, fruit, or other food available by your seat to taste. Can you find "I" in the senses? What if you became blind or deaf? Would part of "me" now be missing, or would "I" still be here? Who is it that perceives or is aware of the objects of sense? Where is this "me" located? Conclusion: "I" cannot be found in the senses or the sense-consciousnesses.

Remember, the goal of this contemplation is to discover and *feel certain* that a singular permanent "self" cannot be found in the skandhas. In fact, even the skandhas themselves are not singular or permanent.

Contemplating "Myself"	
Skandha	**Object of Contemplation**
Form	physical body
Mental formations, including feelings and perceptions	bodily sensations emotional states judgments and opinions names and labels
Consciousness	five sense-consciousnesses the mind that is contemplating the sense of "I"

Contemplating Off the Cushion

Contemplation can be done in the midst of everyday life as well as on the meditation cushion. A meal or simply drinking a glass of water is a good opportunity to experience all five parts of multiplicity. The two tables suggest the points to consider in these contemplations.

Meals	
Form	food, drink, tableware, glasses, linens, etc.
Mental formations, including feeling and perceptions	taste, flavor, smell, touch, texture, sound; opinions, judgments, concepts; names of food and dishes; pleasant or unpleasant
Consciousness	seeing a plate of food, identifying ingredients, and knowing it is dinner

A Glass of Water	
Form	physical glass, water, ice cubes, your body
Mental formations, including feelings and perceptions	Pick up the drinking glass. See its color and material; feel the weight and temperature in your hand, the rim on your lips; drink the water, sensing and tasting it in your mouth and throat. Notice judgments, concepts, pleasantness, or unpleasantness about the drinking glass, water, ice cubes, or your body. Think of object names such as *plastic, water,* and *throat.*
Consciousness	five sense-consciousnesses; mental consciousness that is doing this contemplation; sense of "I"

Contemplation of Suffering

Suffering has two main categories, physical and mental, although we usually experience a mixture of both, with one being stronger. The basis of most mental troubles is the six root kleshas (discussed in chapter 8): ignorance (unawareness of true reality), desire (attachment), anger, pride, doubt, and wrong views. In addition, there are the twenty subsidiary kleshas (see pages 100–102).

The first step to removing suffering is to know how and why we are suffering. Contemplation can help us identify and understand the causes of suffering. If we don't know the causes, actions done to bring pleasure can lead to more suffering.

Suffering is a general term for anything that causes discomfort and a loss of peace. It comes in many forms—small, medium, and large. No one's life is perfect or always easy, and this needs to be accepted, but many areas of suffering can be changed or removed through contemplation. During this exploration of suffering, try to act the part of a kind and curious stranger who is genuinely interested in getting to know you.

It can be helpful to organize suffering into the areas of body, speech, and mind as we identify the forms and causes of our suffering. Suffering of body and mind can often be found even in the Contemplative Meditation session, which should be a time of little or no suffering compared with our daily lives.

Contemplate first the various sufferings that occur through the body. For example, when you are sitting in meditation, physical discomfort such as back pain or a leg falling asleep will often occur.

Then move to speech. How much of the last conversation you had with a friend was pointless chatting or words said to cause harm or unkindness?

End the contemplation session with the sufferings caused by the mind. A case of suffering of the mind occurs when, for instance, you try to contemplate the word "freedom" for one minute but you can't help the intrusion of many other thoughts.

The contemplation of suffering is done so that we understand, and achieve certainty, that we are suffering, in one form or another, almost all the time. Suffering is not confined to extreme incidents of cruelty, despair, injuries, or ruination; it is also the day-in and day-out discomforts like nagging worry, unsatisfied desire, and constant dissatisfaction. Even when we experience a moment of joy, eventually it comes to an end as things change, and this loss causes suffering too. Life in samsara is inherently unsatisfactory, because the only real happiness is found in the realization of lasting peace and enlightenment. Accepting that life is suffering—the first Noble Truth—is not meant to be a cause for depression. Instead, it is the first step in breaking out of depression and finding real happiness.

Suffering is very kind to you. If you don't have suffering, you will not turn from attraction to cyclic existence, which means you will never be free. It's as simple as that.

—Venerable Gyatrul Rinpoche, *Meditation, Transformation, and Dream Yoga*

Contemplation of Emptiness

Experiencing emptiness—the true nature of ourselves, our mind, and reality—is the most powerful antidote for our troubles. It is equated with the peace of nirvana, which frees us from the suffering caused by kleshas and misperceptions. Contemplative Meditation can prepare us to experience the wisdom of emptiness by helping us to understand it conceptually.

Analogies help us gain a concept of what emptiness is. Emptiness is like a mirror, because a mirror can reflect everything, yet the images in a mirror do not truly exist. Emptiness is like a vast space or limitless sky, in which everything that occurs can fit into it most comfortably and in its own place. Emptiness has no existence as a "thing," but it is not nothing. Think of it as the all-encompassing space that allows everything to exist in interdependence. Realize, as Shantideva did, that "Everything is like the sky."

When we use the example of space or sky for emptiness or dharmadhatu it is not the same as the space that is the last of the five elements. This all-encompassing space does not have elements. Here we use the image of space or sky because it is not a "thing." It has no characteristics and impedes nothing.

Ideas for Contemplation

Sit and look around you. Think about what is "here" and what is "there." Stand up and walk a few steps. Now what is "here" and "there" in relation to you? It has changed, hasn't it? At first, "here"

We can only understand the truth of emptiness by contemplating a concept like the self. Placing our mind on this concept and contemplating it is like taking a spaceship to the sun, which is wisdom. As we get closer to the sun, the heat of wisdom ignites the concept. Finally there is no concept, and we realize the empty, ungraspable nature of everything, beyond the four extremes of existence, nonexistence, neither, or both. This is how we arrive at an understanding of emptiness. There is no way that concept can land on wisdom, but we have to use concept to get there.

—SAKYONG MIPHAM RINPOCHE, *Ruling Your World*

---

was in the place where you were sitting, and "there" was at a distance from your bodily presence. But when you walked over to "there," then "there" became "here"!

Write the word HERE on a piece of paper. Put the piece of paper down where you are sitting or standing, and think, "I am putting this paper *here*." Then move back a few steps and look at the paper with the word HERE on it. What happened? HERE has become *there*. Do "here" and "there" actually exist? Yes, "here" and "there" exist—but it depends on where *you* sit or stand.

The same is true for left and right. If you drive eastward on a freeway, then the road in front is east; yet in a few moments of driving, it is west of you. This is a simple and easy way to begin to notice that what is true for here and there, left and right, or east and west is true for everything. It all depends on your reference point.

Pick up an object close at hand. Look at it, rotate it, turn it over and upside down, looking carefully at it each time. Notice the differences that occur with each change in orientation. Look at it very closely to see how much has changed just by moving it. Briefly identify the different parts and materials of the object. Consider how it might look under a microscope at higher and higher powers until you reach the atomic or subatomic level. At this level all the qualities associated with the object are long gone.

Compare thinking, dreams, waking life, and movies. You can "lose" yourself in your thoughts, a good book, or a movie. Dreams use all of your senses and are filled with vivid imagery and emotional content. They seem so real that sometimes when you wake up, you can't believe it was "only a dream"; yet the dream has vanished, and in a few moments you may be unable to remember a single detail. We all have a strong belief that this waking life is "real" and these other phenomena are not; but consider: how is your waking life different from thinking, dreaming, or watching a movie?

These are some ideas for your contemplation session. At the end of the session, remember to dedicate the merit.

Heart Sutra Practice

To deepen your understanding of emptiness, I encourage you to read the brief Heart Sutra translation presented in part five, along with a line-by-line commentary and further suggestions for practice and chanting. Work with the sutra to further your intellectual understanding of emptiness and help you aspire to experience emptiness by means of meditation.

The Heart Sutra is the best known of Shakyamuni Buddha's teachings on emptiness. It is a favorite brief text throughout the Asian countries where the Mahayana school of Buddhism is practiced. Traditionally it is believed that when you read a sutra, either silently or aloud, you are making a good karmic connection with the speech of the Buddha. For this reason, many laypeople as well as monks and nuns, individually and in groups, chant the Heart Sutra. When I lived at Namdroling Monastery in South India, we chanted the Heart Sutra every morning during the traditional summer retreat. The sound of thousands of monks chanting together in Tibetan was like a waterfall after spring rains.

Although the text is quite short, it is very profound, giving a deep understanding of our true nature and the nature of reality. There are three steps to deepening your understanding of emptiness through study of the Heart Sutra. First is *hearing*, which means to listen to teachings and study the texts and commentaries. Next is *contemplation*, thinking about what you understand from your listening and reading. The third step is *meditation*, which means letting go of the words while holding the understanding in your mind. All three come together in the practice of chanting. See the instructions in "Practices to Deepen Understanding of the Heart Sutra," beginning on page 202.

Conclusion

This book is like a meritorious person who has found a way to create a happy life for him- or herself. It has a form like a body. It is filled with words about feelings, perceptions, formations, and consciousnesses. These are the ingredients that, when combined together, create a person. According to the Buddha Dharma we have to know ourselves very well. We are impermanent, we are made of separate things put together, we have troubles and suffering—and also we have the innate potential to find peace and happiness.

This path that leads to a happy life can be found and followed. It is walked through our actions, our words, and mainly our thoughts. Mistaken beliefs and views, misbehaviors, and improper ways of speech are the root causes of suffering and trouble. This is not hidden from any of us if we look carefully at ourselves and those around us.

It is the rare person who can change immediately. Your mind can teach you a great deal, but without a living human teacher it is difficult to fully understand the nature of reality. The Dharma teacher introduces us to the realities of life and the nature of our mind. It is the job of the teacher to show the right path through teaching and being a role model.

Initially, although you may go through the steps found in this book, it won't seem to do very much to change your ego-clinging or your desire to hold on to "me" and "mine." This habit is extremely strong. But if you can persist in the contemplations, returning to them again and again—both in formal meditation and in everyday life—you will notice that your perception of a solid "I" gradually becomes weaker and weaker.

You can and should be able to gauge your progress and know that this path of Contemplative Meditation is working. When your understanding gets closer to the truth, your mind will naturally relax, resulting in less mental stress and emotional upheaval. To get to this place, we all have a lot of gentle but thorough work to do. Luckily, there are plenty of useful opportunities to examine, investigate, and contemplate. All the happenings that arise naturally in daily living become our place of meditation.

I cannot say this too strongly, as it is the key to becoming a great meditator with a changed life: In the beginning, when your meditation is not clear, do not become discouraged and depressed, thinking you don't have the knowledge, the luck, the qualities, or whatever is necessary to do this well. Our habitual patterns of thinking and our misperceptions are very strong. We cannot change years and lifetimes of habit, so deeply ingrained in the psyche, in a few sessions.

Keep going by creating a regular practice, and don't forget. Just as your body needs to eat every day, in the same way your mind hungers to be at ease and needs the food of meditation. Successful meditators find and use the proper methods. This book gives you some methods, but you must do the daily work.

As spoken by the Buddha to his disciples:

I have shown you the path to liberation.
You must know that liberation depends on you.

Contemplation Checklist

√ It is not enough to just read or listen to the teachings; we must contemplate them.

√ Even a moment's reflection on the Four Seals is beneficial, because they contain the entirety of the Buddha's teachings.

√ Contemplation and analysis lead to knowledge of our true nature.

√ When obscurations fall away, your true, unchanging nature of happiness and peace is revealed.

√ Wisdom arising from contemplation leads to the dissolving of habits patterns, misperceptions, and disturbing emotions.

√ Use the remembrance of precious human birth and impermanence as a spur to joyful effort and faithful practice.

√ Change will happen over time as you turn the wheel of analysis again and again.

Part Five

Readings

The Heart Sutra

The Sutra of the Heart of Transcendent Knowledge

Thus have I heard. Once the Blessed One was dwelling in Rajagrha
at Vulture Peak Mountain, together with a great gathering of the
sangha of monks and a great gathering of the sangha of bodhisattvas. At that time the Blessed One entered the samadhi that expresses the dharma called "profound illumination," and at the same
time noble Avalokiteshvara, the bodhisattva mahasattva, while practicing the profound prajnaparamita, saw in this way: he saw the five
skandhas to be empty of nature.

Then, through the power of the Buddha, venerable Shariputra
said to noble Avalokiteshvara, the bodhisattva mahasattva, "How
should a son or daughter of noble family train, who wishes to
practice the profound prajnaparamita?"

Addressed in this way, noble Avalokiteshvara, the bodhisattva
mahasattva, said to venerable Shariputra, "O Shariputra, a son or
daughter of noble family who wishes to practice the profound
prajnaparamita should see in this way: seeing the five skandhas
to be empty of nature. Form is emptiness; emptiness also is form.
Emptiness is no other than form; form is no other than emptiness.
In the same way, feeling, perception, formation, and consciousness

are emptiness. Thus, Shariputra, all dharmas are emptiness. There are no characteristics. There is no birth and no cessation. There is no impurity and no purity. There is no decrease and no increase. Therefore, Shariputra, in emptiness, there is no form, no feeling, no perception, no formation, no consciousness; no eye, no ear, no nose, no tongue, no body, no mind; no appearance, no sound, no smell, no taste, no touch, no dharmas; no eye dhatu up to no mind dhatu, no dhatu of dharmas, no mind consciousness dhatu; no ignorance, no end of ignorance up to no old age and death, no end of old age and death; no suffering, no origin of suffering, no cessation of suffering, no path, no wisdom, no attainment, and no nonattainment. Therefore, Shariputra, since the bodhisattvas have no attainment, they abide by means of prajnaparamita. Since there is no obscuration of mind, there is no fear. They transcend falsity and attain complete nirvana. All the buddhas of the three times, by means of prajnaparamita, fully awaken to unsurpassable, true, complete enlightenment. Therefore, the great mantra of prajnaparamita, the mantra of great insight, the unsurpassed mantra, the unequaled mantra, the mantra that calms all suffering, should be known as truth, since there is no deception. The prajnaparamita mantra is said in this way:

OM GATE GATE PARAGATE PARASAMGATE BODHI SVAHA

Thus, Shariputra, the bodhisattva mahasattva should train in the profound prajnaparamita."

Then the Blessed One arose from that samadhi and praised noble Avalokiteshvara, the bodhisattva mahasattva, saying, "Good, good, O son of noble family; thus it is, O son of noble family, thus it is. One should practice the profound prajnaparamita just as you have taught and all the tathagatas will rejoice."

When the Blessed One had said this, venerable Shariputra and noble Avalokiteshvara, the bodhisattva mahasattva, that whole assembly and the world with its gods, humans, asuras, and gandharvas rejoiced and praised the words of the Blessed One.

....

Lotsawa Bhikshu Rinchen De translated this text into Tibetan with the Indian pandita Vimalamitra. It was edited by the great editor-lotsawas Gelong, Namkha, and others. This Tibetan text was copied from the fresco in Gegye Chemaling at the glorious Samye vihara.

Avalokiteshvara, the Bodhisattva of Compassion

Shariputra, disciple of the Buddha

A Commentary on the Heart Sutra

Emptiness is no other than form; form is no other than emptiness.

Introduction

The Heart Sutra is the distilled essence of a specific group of Mahayana sutras called the *Prajnaparamita Sutras,* grouped together because they all concern the wisdom (*prajna*) that "reaches the other shore" (*paramita*). This wisdom is called the Mother of Buddhas. When one thinks of the mother, it is she who gives birth. Without a mother there can be no child. In the same way, when we consider the buddhas of the past, present, and future, we can ask: where did they all come from? Their mother is the Prajnaparamita alone. Without the realization of prajnaparamita, the "perfection of wisdom," there are no buddhas. Wisdom is the ability to directly know and experience the fundamental nature of all phenomena, which is emptiness.

The full Sanskrit title of the Heart Sutra is *Prajnaparamita Hridaya Sutra* (the Sutra of the Heart of Transcendent Knowledge). The term *prajnaparamita* refers to the transcendent virtue (paramita) of wisdom or knowledge (prajna), one of the six paramitas of a bodhisattva.

The Heart Sutra is the most popular and commonly recited sutra in Mahayana Buddhist countries, chanted by both monastic and lay practitioners, individually and in groups. Every Tibetan New Year, to remove obstacles for families and communities, all one hundred thousand verses of the *Prajnaparamita Sutra* are chanted. With twelve monastic chanters reciting simultaneously, it takes about fifteen hours to complete. Nowadays most people do not have the time to practice for hours, but the Heart Sutra can be recited in about five minutes. Even though it is short, yet it is profound and vast in meaning.

These most celebrated of the Buddha's teachings on emptiness are presented in the form of a dialogue between Avalokiteshvara and Shariputra. Avalokiteshvara is the Bodhisattva of Compassion, and Shariputra is a close disciple of the Buddha.

Shariputra came from a Hindu brahmin family and had already started a spiritual life when he encountered the teachings of the Buddha. After hearing about the Dharma from a monk named Assaji, one of the Buddha's first five students, Shariputra sought out the Buddha and also became his student. Shariputra often taught with the Buddha's approval and was one of the most highly praised of his disciples. He is central to many teachings in the sutras.

Although the Mahayana sutras are considered to be the words of the Buddha, those words sometimes come through other buddhas or bodhisattvas. Thus, although the Buddha does not participate in the dialogue described in this sutra, he is in a deep state of meditative concentration (*samadhi* in Sanskrit), in which he inspires in Avalokiteshvara a profound realization that the five skandhas are empty of any self-existence. The Buddha also inspires Shariputra to ask the question that starts the dialogue. Avalokiteshvara then becomes the Buddha's spokesperson for presenting the teachings on emptiness to Shariputra.

The Bodhisattva of Compassion

Avalokiteshvara is like the moon
Whose cool light puts out the burning fires of samsara.
In its rays the night-flowering lotus of compassion
Opens wide its petals.
   —quoted in *The Tibetan Book of Living and Dying*
      by Sogyal Rinpoche

Compassion manifests in our world as Avalokiteshvara, known in Tibetan as Chenrezig. The Bodhisattva of Compassion vowed to delay his own enlightenment in order to help liberate all other beings first. He is invoked under different names and in different forms, both male and female, depending on the country or the type of Buddhism practiced. In East Asia, for example, she is Kuan Yin or Kannon, who hears the cries of all sentient beings in times of difficulty.

Historical folklore of Tibet tells how an emanation of Avalokiteshvara named Old Monkey Bodhisattva was the ancestor of the Tibetan people. Similarly, the Dalai Lamas are revered as human emanations of the Bodhisattva of Compassion.

The mantra of Avalokiteshvara, OM MANI PADME HUM, is the primary mantra of Tibet. Tibetans learn the six-syllable Mani mantra as they learn their first words, and it is a thread throughout their lives. It is recited, carved on stones, painted on objects and buildings, and written on paper used to fill prayer wheels, statues, and stupas.

Reciting the mantra prevents rebirth in the six realms by purifying the karma that would lead to being born in samsara, and at the same time purifies the suffering inherent in each realm. OM MANI PADME HUM, recited wholeheartedly, strengthens the ability to perfect the six paramitas: generosity, ethics, patience, joyous effort, meditative concentration, and wisdom. It is a protection from negative influences and some forms of illness.

Traditional Historical Views

The Heart Sutra is part of the Sutra tradition that preserves the original words of the Buddha. Gathering these oral teachings and establishing them in written form was a long process that began right after his death.

The Buddha's death—known as his *parinirvana*, his passing into complete nirvana—occurred more than twenty-five hundred years ago. It is said that eighty million arhats, his disciples who had reached the highest level, also passed away at the same time as the Buddha. Prior to the Buddha's passing, Maudgalyayana, one of the Buddha's two main disciples during his lifetime (along with Shariputra), as well as seventy thousand arhats had already passed away.

Tradition tells that with the passing of the Buddha and so many great arhats, the gods were saying that the example and teachings of the Buddha Shakyamuni would no longer be clearly and authentically present in this world, but would be "like smoke from a dead fire." To prevent this from happening, the First Buddhist Council, consisting of five hundred arhats, assembled a year after the Buddha's parinirvana and collected all of his teachings. The three presiding arhats at the council were Upali, the oldest disciple; Ananda, the Buddha's cousin and personal attendant; and Mahakashyapa, the most learned of the disciples. Each of them recited the Buddha's teachings and discourses, which they had learned by heart.

The teachings were divided into three sections, which became known as the Tripitaka, literally three "baskets": the Vinaya-pitaka is the collection on moral discipline for monks and nuns, recited by Upali; the Sutra-pitaka is the collection of major discourses, recited by Ananda; and the Abhidharma-pitaka is the collection of metaphysical teachings, repeated by Mahakashyapa.

One hundred and ten years later, the Second Buddhist Council took place, with an assembly of seven hundred arhats. Due to arguments and debates about the Vinaya rules, this council met to recite the Buddha's teachings and to remember them accurately.

Over two hundred years later, five hundred arhats and five thousand monks met in the Third Buddhist Council. By this time, eighteen schools had developed, each with a slightly different way of chanting the Vinaya-pitaka. The arhats were able to remember and recite the teachings, so they had been transmitting them orally to their students. This is why all sutras begin with the phrase, "Thus have I heard. Once . . ."

Up until this time, some sutras and Abhidharma teachings had been written down, but not the Buddha's teachings of the Vinaya-pitaka. When the Third Council was over, all of the Buddha's teachings had been both validated and written down.

There is also a second, legendary history within the Mahayana traditions that says the ones who actually compiled the Buddha's teachings were the bodhisattvas Vajrapani, Manjushri, and Maitreya. This history recounts that about two hundred years after the Buddha's parinirvana, one million bodhisattvas gathered, along with these three great bodhisattvas, south of Rajagrha on the top of Vimalasvabhava Mountain, and compiled the Mahayana teachings of the Buddha.

Traditionally it is said that Maitreya compiled the Vinaya-pitaka, Manjushri the Sutra-pitaka, and Vajrapani compiled the Abhidharma-pitaka—the three collections of the Buddha's teachings that are together called the Tripitaka. After these teachings were written down, they were then taken many places in different realms, including the human, god, and naga realms.

This tradition also asserts that six hundred years after the parinirvana of the Buddha (second century C.E.), the great master Nagarjuna brought the 100,000-verse *Prajnaparamita Sutra* from the naga realm. The original text he brought back can be seen in Kathmandu, Nepal. It is said that the place where this text is kept is the doorway to the naga realm where Nagarjuna went to receive it. It is on this sutra that Nagarjuna based the Middle Way philosophy of the Madhyamaka school, which is considered the best presentation of the wisdom of emptiness.

The Prajnaparamita Teachings

There are four well-known versions of the *Prajnaparamita Sutras:* the long version (100,000 verses); the medium version (20,000 verses); the short version (8,000 verses); and the Heart Sutra. The Heart Sutra is the briefest, a summary reflecting the essence of these profound teachings, and primarily emphasizes emptiness.

The term *prajnaparamita* consists of the words *prajna* and *paramita. Prajna* is sometimes translated as "discriminating awareness." The Tibetan term is *sherab,* "supreme knowing," or the most sublime way of knowing. What prajna knows is emptiness. True experiences of emptiness will simultaneously include the arising of the great warmth of compassion.

The word *paramita* implies crossing over to the other shore of both samsara and nirvana. Nirvana, in this case, is the nirvana of the Hinayana, which is one of the two general divisions of Buddhism. *Hinayana* is a collective term for the eighteen Buddhist schools referred to earlier. Hinayana is often called "the lesser vehicle" because the motivation is lesser than in Mahayana. The motivation of Hinayana practitioners is renunciation of samsara, and their goal is personal nirvana. There are two kinds of Hinayana practitioners: shravakas (hearers) and pratyekabuddhas (solitary-realizers).

It is important to note that the shravakas' and pratyekabuddhas' nirvana is not the same as the Mahayana concept of nirvana. The nirvana of a buddha is beyond samsara and the Hinayana Buddhist's nirvana. From the Mahayana point of view, the nirvana of the shravakas and pratyekabuddhas is not complete, because there are still very subtle cognitive obscurations that have not yet been purified.

Shravakas listened to their teachers with a motivation to become arhats and achieve their own liberation. Pratyekabuddhas are buddhas who remain in seclusion and do not teach the Dharma to others by means of words. Pratyekabuddhas are not "perfectly enlightened buddhas" (*samyaksambuddhas*), because they lack bodhichitta.

As the goal of spiritual practice in Hinayana Buddhism, nirvana means liberation from the cycle of rebirth and the end of suffering. This nirvana is a cessation of all samsaric phenomena made of the compounded skandhas. It comes through understanding selflessness.

The combination *prajna* and *paramita* connotes the most sublime way of knowing that culminates in crossing to the other shore of samsara and nirvana. This "other shore" is the Mahayana nirvana. Nirvana is our buddha-nature completely manifesting without any obscurations or doubts. There is no "place" outside of you that you go to when nirvana is realized, since nirvana is our basic, fundamental, indwelling nature.

Prajnaparamita has two different aspects: subject and object. The subject is wisdom, which is the ability to know the fundamental nature of all phenomena directly and is the primary focus of prajnaparamita. The object is great emptiness—that is, realizing buddha-nature, the fundamental nature of all phenomena, which is simplicity, or freedom from elaboration. "Elaboration" in this context means concepts, words, things, and all phenomenal existence.

The Prajnaparamita literature, and especially the Heart Sutra, teaches the subject, in this case ourselves, as being empty. From the point of view of the fundamental nature, there isn't any differentiation between subject and object. Traditionally, however, it is taught in terms of having these two viewpoints, subject as wisdom and object as emptiness.

Subject and object can be considered through the teachings of Nagarjuna and Maitreya. The teachings of Nagarjuna focus on the "great emptiness" aspect of all phenomena. The teachings of Maitreya focus on the wisdom mind that leads to an understanding of this emptiness.

There is also a direct meaning and an implied meaning within the *Prajnaparamita Sutras* that is expressed eloquently in the writings of these two teachers. Nagarjuna sees all phenomena as empty, and this is considered to be the "direct meaning" of the *Prajnaparamita Sutras*. The implied meaning taught by Maitreya is compassion, bodhichitta, the wisdom that sees selflessness, and omniscience. (A recommended work combining the teachings of Nagarjuna and Maitreya is *The Adornment of the Middle Way: Shantarakshita's "Madhyamakalankara,"* with commentary by Jamgon Mipham, translated by the Padmakara Translation Group.)

There are three traditional ways of explaining prajnaparamita: ground prajnaparamita, path prajnaparamita, and fruition prajnaparamita.

Ground prajnaparamita is the fundamental nature of all phenomena. Free from complexity or elaboration, it is the union of emptiness and clarity beyond word and concept.

Emptiness does not mean that nothing whatsoever exists; it means that all appearance or form is without a separate, self-existent identity. Emptiness is not a "thing"; it is the absence of inherent or true existence in all phenomena. Emptiness is complete openness without obstruction that allows everything to occur. Therefore, emptiness and phenomena are really one. "Apparent yet empty; empty yet apparent" is an often-used phrase. As you look more deeply into existence, over time an understanding of this saying will grow within you.

Path prajnaparamita is the wisdom that understands, through direct realization, the fundamental nature of all phenomena. This direct understanding is the beginning of the path of seeing because one now has clear insight or an experience of the fundamental nature. Bodhisattvas on this path continue to develop more profound and vast qualities as they progress from the first through the tenth stages, or bhumis. The Sanskrit word for stage or level is *bhumi,* literally "earth" or "ground." Just as the ground is the support for everything, both animate and inanimate, the bhumis are said to be "supports" for enlightened qualities. This term is used when referring to the stages a bodhisattva traverses on the path to enlightenment. This is how the fundamental nature of our mind is actualized and how it manifests.

There are ten bhumis in the Mahayana: Complete Joy, Immaculate/Stainless, Luminous/Illuminating, Radiant, Hard to Keep/Hard to Conquer, Clearly Manifest, Far Progressed, Immovable, Perfect Intellect, and Cloud of Dharma. The eleventh bhumi, Universal Radiance, is buddhahood. The ten bhumis are part of the five paths, which is another way of describing the journey to enlightenment: (1) The path of accumulation is reached when we realize bodhichitta. (2) The path of preparation is the deepening of our understanding of reality and emptiness. (3) The path of seeing is a direct realization of emptiness, and at this time a practitioner becomes an arya and is on the first bhumi. (4) The path of meditation uses insight gained from the path of seeing to further remove obscurations; this path is the progression from the second bhumi through the tenth bhumi. (5) The path of no more learning is the achievement of nirvana; it means becoming an arhat on the Hinayana path or achieving buddhahood on the Mahayana path.

Fruition prajnaparamita is the full and complete actualization of the wisdom that is the direct realization of the nature of all phenomena. This is the wisdom of buddhahood and complete freedom from suffering.

Line-by-Line Commentary

In ancient India, there were two main Buddhist monastic universities: Vikramashila and Nalanda. From the Nalanda tradition comes the way of explaining the sutras called the five perfect conditions: the teacher, the student (or retinue), the time, the place, and the teaching. This commentary on the Heart Sutra is organized on the principles of the five perfect conditions: perfect time, perfect student, perfect teacher, perfect place, and perfect sangha (retinue, or community of Buddhist practitioners).

The sutra begins:

Thus have I heard. Once the Blessed One . . .

All sutras begin with the phrase *"Thus have I heard. Once . . ."* The word *once* refers to the perfect condition of time when the teaching was given by the Buddha. The audience listening to the teachings at that time is considered to exhibit the perfect condition of the student or retinue. This audience did not write these teachings down but had the capability to listen to the Buddha's words and remember them completely.

The Blessed One is the Buddha, who exhibits the perfect condition of teacher. The Buddha abandoned all kleshas and attained all virtuous qualities. He completely transcended all of samsara and nirvana. These three qualities of the Blessed One make the Buddha the perfect teacher. The perfect condition of the teacher tells us what qualities of the Buddha we should think about (as discussed earlier in the visualization section) and aspire to envision within ourselves.

The Sanskrit word translated as "Blessed One" is *bhagavan*. Its Tibetan equivalent, *chomdende*, is significant because *chom* means to tame, subdue, or subjugate. The Buddha subdued the four *maras*, or negative influences: the mara of the kleshas, the mara of the skandhas, the mara of the Lord of Death, and the mara of indolence. The word *den* means to possess, and what is possessed are the six paramitas (see pages 61–62). The Buddha possessed the prajnaparamita, or supreme omniscience. *De* means transcend, and here it means that the Buddha has passed beyond samsara and nirvana. Here *nirvana* refers to the nirvana of the shravakas and pratyekabuddhas, not that of the Mahayana.

. . . was dwelling in Rajagrha at Vulture Peak Mountain together with a great gathering of the sangha of monks and a great gathering of the sangha of bodhisattvas.

Vulture Peak Mountain refers to the perfect place, or location, where the teaching actually occurred. It is in the region of Bodhgaya in what was central India, near Nalanda University, an important place of learning not only for Hinayana and Mahayana philosophy but also for logic, medicine, astrology, and many other subjects. Vulture Peak is one of the major Buddhist pilgrimage sites in India.

Those who were listening to these teachings—the bodhisattvas, monks, nuns, gods, nagas, and other beings—exhibit the perfect condition of the retinue, or sangha.

A great gathering of the sangha of monks refers to the monastic community of both monks and nuns. As a monastic, one takes up the path of virtue, so the focus is on actually practicing virtue. In Tibetan *gelong* means to take up the path of virtue and is the term for a fully ordained monk. A fully ordained nun is called a *gelongma*.

The second phrase, *a great gathering of the sangha of bodhisattvas*, applies to great practitioners who have genuine awakened mind, or bodhichitta. Within that context, not only are they listening to the Dharma teachings and practicing virtue in that way, but they have a direct realization of the true nature.

Bodhisattvas come into all the realms of existence in many forms, but their great kindness and willingness to help sentient beings is universal. Some become well known and others are known to a few. Most are not recognized by the sentient beings who receive their help.

At that time the Blessed One entered the samadhi that expresses the dharma called "profound illumination" ...

The perfect condition of the time occurred when all these different groups of beings, as well as the Buddha, came together for this teaching. The perfect condition of the teaching occurred when the Buddha entered the samadhi, or meditative state, of the inseparable union of appearance-emptiness, and out of that state this teaching was given.

... and at the same time noble Avalokiteshvara, the bodhisattva mahasattva, while practicing the profound prajnaparamita, saw in this way ...

When the Buddha entered into samadhi, Avalokiteshvara was blessed and was thus able to attain the same understanding and realization as the Buddha. The Blessed One was not actually reciting this teaching, but was present in a meditative state that expressed this profoundly illuminating insight, the samadhi of appearance-emptiness.

This meditative state of equipoise is beyond concepts or words. In this state of wisdom awareness, you have confidence in—and a direct knowing beyond doubt of—that which is named emptiness, non-arising and noncessation, unborn, one taste, or without reference point. This samadhi of appearance-emptiness can only be described with words like the preceding, or as space-like. Space is without form, feeling, color, shape, direction, or reference point. As a common teaching says, "A mute person can eat candy but cannot tell anyone else about the experience."

The text then goes on presenting what Avalokiteshvara actually saw:

... he saw the five skandhas to be empty of nature.

Then, through the power of the Buddha, venerable Shariputra said to noble Avalokiteshvara, the bodhisattva mahasattva, "How should a son or daughter of noble family train, who wishes to practice the profound prajnaparamita?"

Then, through the Buddha's blessing, venerable Shariputra had the courage or heart to ask a question regarding emptiness. Shariputra does not directly ask the Buddha, since the Buddha is in samadhi, but he does ask Avalokiteshvara about this meditation on emptiness. This is what the text describes. Here, Shariputra is thinking about present and future students and how they should meditate on emptiness.

The Meditation on Emptiness

Addressed in this way, noble Avalokiteshvara, the bodhisattva mahasattva, said to venerable Shariputra, "O Shariputra, a son or daughter of noble family who wishes to practice the profound prajnaparamita should see in this way: seeing the five skandhas to be empty of nature. Form is emptiness; emptiness also is form. Emptiness is no other than form; form is no other than emptiness. In the same way, feeling, perception, formation, and consciousness are emptiness."

Avalokiteshvara responds to Shariputra's question by stating clearly that these parts, the five skandhas that we take as a whole and consider to be ourselves, are not truly existent. In this reply it is also understood that the self or "I" does not truly exist either.

These five skandhas are the five heaps or aggregates that make up our being. They come together at birth and separate at death. The five aggregates are form, which includes all physical things; feeling, which is grouped in the three main categories of pleasant, unpleasant, and neutral; perception, which specifically characterizes the features of an object (shape, color, etc.); formation, which is all concepts affecting an experience that are not included in the other four skandhas; and consciousness, which is the mind that is aware of things and is generally divided into awareness of vision, sounds, smells, taste, touch, and mind.

Avalokiteshvara says that all the forms we perceive are empty of any inherent nature. Usually we think of the phenomena of the world as being either real and substantial or not real and not substantial. We cling to objects that we think are real or substantial. We don't cling to objects that we think are not real or substantial. There is a connection between clinging to things as real and the understanding of emptiness. The more we understand emptiness, the less we hold on to things, events, and people as being unchanging, substantial, other, or "mine."

When we realize emptiness, we realize that all phenomena are pervaded by emptiness, meaning that things are not as they appear through our senses. Through the energy or manifestation of emptiness, there is the appearance of form. Modern science and technology have revealed that forms, when viewed at the microscopic, atomic, and subatomic levels, lose the attributes that we conventionally give to objects, such as solidity and substantiality. For example, when we view a table at the atomic or subatomic level we see that it is largely made up of space. Thus a table appears solid but in fact is not.

We can experience something similar on our computers when

we take photo-editing software and zoom into a picture with the highest magnification. The picture loses its shape, becomes pixels of color, and then even the pixels lose distinct color qualities.

Consider our own bodies arising from the meeting of microscopic egg and sperm and the subsequent coming together of genetic material. When we become familiar with the stages of development of the human body, we understand that we are not, and never have been, one lasting and static entity from conception through death and then decay.

We are made up of many parts. Like a water glass, we have a conventional bottom and top, inside and outside, left and right sides. Under a microscope we can see the finer and finer constituents of the body such as cells and DNA. We can then ask: Where does the notion of body actually reside? Does it reside in these finer and finer constituents, or does it reside in our feelings and thoughts connected with our bodily form? What is the feeling that we associate with our bodily form? What do we identify with and hold to be dear?

Let us consider our feelings and thoughts associated with "I" or ego. Usually we don't think about it, but when we do, we think of ourselves as substantial or permanently existing. If we break down this "I," it consists of our form, our feelings, our perceptions, our mental formations, and our consciousness. These, the five skandhas, are blended together and labeled "I." There is no permanent or transient self that can be found separate from the five skandhas.

Our sense of "I" began before we were born when our parents picked out our name. Over and over, from birth, we have heard our name and gender repeated. This has reinforced a pattern of attachment to self and body. Thus the "I" of this lifetime begins. We have the patterns of being human and we have the patterns of each lifetime. All have come about in this same way.

Speech and thoughts are other areas of self-identification that need to be analyzed carefully, asking if anything substantial or existing can be found in the patterns of speech and in the myriad of thoughts.

The root cause of the suffering we experience is this strong belief in a true and permanent self. The antidote to clinging to the existence of ourselves, with all its hope and fear, is the knowledge of emptiness.

From a conventional or worldly point of view, it is valid and reasonable to say that this singular "I" exists. Conventionally we identify and name ourselves, other sentient beings, plants, minerals, and objects. When we have discussions with others, we talk about an "I" or "me." Buddhism acknowledges that the five skandhas we label "I" exist conventionally. However, from an ultimate point of view, this "I" does not exist. The view presented in the prajnaparamita teachings is ultimate.

With the Buddha's teachings, one needs to analyze very carefully this conventional and ultimate "I." Think in depth about who you think you are. We can start by thinking about form in a gross or rough way, as opposed to a subtle way. When we think of the couplet *Form is emptiness; emptiness also is form*, it is somewhat easy for us to understand that form is emptiness. If we analyze and break form down into pieces, we can see that there is nothing singular and unchanging. There is always a way to further subdivide the ever-changing parts.

The activities of taking things apart and looking carefully at the microscopic, atomic, and subatomic levels show the nonexistence of solid forms and give a clearer understanding of this truth. We can apply our understanding of emptiness of form to the other four skandhas: feeling, perception, mental formations, and consciousness. The antidote of emptiness will disperse the incorrect notion that the five skandhas are real and permanently existing.

We all experience the existence of forms. It's more difficult to see that emptiness is also form. "Interdependence" is a way of expressing this underlying quality of energy pervading all that exists. Everything is always changing, yet forms arise, dwell, and cease in their place and time. This mysterious emptiness that is everywhere is not easily understood. The study of astronomy, biology, and botany can strengthen an appreciation of the teaching "emptiness is form." From the vastness of the cosmos to the space within matter seen under the microscope, the unity of emptiness and matter becomes obvious in the sciences.

It is important to remember that the understandings discussed in the Heart Sutra are from the ultimate point of view realized by the Buddha. It's not necessarily something that is within our own current understanding or point of view. Typically we do not see form as emptiness, so we need to seriously think about and analyze this. Why is form emptiness, and what does this mean?

The example of a chariot was used in olden times to analyze this idea. So let us update it and take the example of a car. If we take a car apart, we will have thousands of things made of different materials, of different sizes, shapes, weights, colors, and so on. Can we find "car" in its parts? We might say the car is the sum of its parts. But the question of what is a "car" still remains. We could consider all the way down to the atoms themselves, but then we've further lost the concept of car because we've gone beyond parts and are now thinking of atoms. We know from a scientific point of view that atoms can be broken down into parts as well, as subatomic particles.

In a similar way we can think of our favorite football team. Typically, when our team wins, we feel great. We'll want to celebrate with our friends and have a nice party. On the other hand, when our favorite team loses, we may get depressed and frustrated. On the big loss days, we may feel angry, get into arguments, or even worse. But when we think of football teams these days, it's difficult to pin down what really makes up a team. The players come and go, and sometimes the players on a particular team will be substantially different from one season to the next. The coaches and owners also come and go. New stadiums are built, uniforms change, and sometimes the teams are moved from one town to another. At times, the only thing about a team that doesn't change is the team's name. When we think of our favorite football team in this way, we realize that it's somewhat of a facade. It doesn't really exist in any substantive way. At the same time, it's difficult not to be attached to our favorite football team.

We can extend this line of thought to our favorite schools, organizations, nations, and so on. In doing so, we begin to see that all of our solid notions of reality are marked by a combination of emptiness and appearance.

Let us take as another example of emptiness, the basic Buddhist doctrine of karma, cause and effect. From the ultimate point of view, nothing ever happens—there is no substantial or independent occurrence. At the same time, from the relative point of view, karma is the cause for the existence of the realms of samsara.

Nagarjuna in the *Precious Garland* (*Ratnavali*) expressed this in one stanza:

As long as one clings to the skandhas
There will be clinging to self.
If there is clinging to self, there will be karma.
And from karma there will be rebirth.

When we think about it in this way, the car, the football team, the atom, karma, ourselves, and so on, all of which we usually think of as being here or having some importance, really doesn't exist in a sense. None of them has a substantial, permanent existence, yet they appear and we can see them. This is what is meant by *"Form is emptiness."* This is true of all phenomena. We think of all things as substantially existing and being solid, but this is not the case.

This is how we can think about and analyze emptiness, since we don't yet have a direct experience of emptiness. We have to think about it, and analyze our experience of solidity and this "thingness" quality of phenomena that we experience. Then we will gain an understanding of emptiness.

It is important to do this because it is the inseparability of emptiness and appearances that allows everything we accept as our daily life to occur. All appearances, all phenomena and sentient beings (including ourselves), have this quality of being empty of a solid, unified existence. This emptiness creates the space for things to happen and gives us the ability to change.

Our name is a strong habitual pattern and an object of grasping as a substantial part of what makes up "I." If we realize that our name is no more than a helpful conceptual designation, we can begin to see all the other concepts that we habitually take as truth and grasp as real and part of ourselves, needing to be defended.

Suppose our partner or child comes into our presence. Unpleasant feelings of grasping, jealousy, or possessiveness might arise within us. We have these feelings because we believe that this person is real and the relationship with us is real. However, if we recognize that the person and the relationship don't truly exist in a substantial way and are always changing just like ourselves, then these negative emotional attachments are more likely to disperse.

Attachment is one example of the afflictive emotions. There are other kleshas, such as anger, pride, jealousy, envy, and passion. Perhaps we get into a vicious argument with a person and we stop being friends. At that time, if we understand that everything is empty of true existence, we won't regard the person, ourselves, or the anger as substantial. As a result, we won't be so caught up in our own negative emotion. Sometimes people are friends, stop being friends, and then later they may become friends again. Relationships are always changing.

Emptiness is an antidote to all the kleshas. From this point of view, we see the emptiness within emotions in the same way we see emptiness within appearances. Emptiness is the true nature of all phenomena. An immediate benefit of even a little understanding is a reduction of suffering.

The truth of emptiness is powerful and dispels confusion. Shantideva in the *Bodhicharyavatara* said:

Emptiness is the antidote
To the darkness of the emotional and cognitive
    obscurations.
How could those who seek omniscience
Fail to meditate on this at once?

Again, emptiness isn't something that can be differentiated from a form: *Emptiness is no other than form; form is no other than emptiness.* Form and emptiness have never been, and cannot be, separated or divided. Form is not on one side and emptiness on the other and we're trying to glue them together. They are inseparable and cannot be divided from each other. Like the reflections in a mirror, all exists yet does not exist.

One example of the actual experience of the inseparability of form and emptiness is found in the life of Tibet's great yogi, Milarepa. Through the profoundness of his realization he was unobstructed by phenomena. When we touch a wall, it is an obstruction to us. It's solid. But Milarepa could actually walk through walls. He could walk through rocks, go underneath the ground, and fly up in the air. We know that his direct realization of emptiness was complete because there was no obstruction of form.

Avalakitoshvara goes on:

Thus, Shariputra, all dharmas are emptiness. There are no characteristics.

The word *dharma* has several meanings (see the glossary). Usually it refers to spiritual teachings, mainly those of Shakyamuni Buddha. Here, when Avalokiteshvara tells Shariputra that all dharmas are emptiness, *dharma* means all phenomena. All factors of the experienced world as we experience it, all phenomena with definable characteristics, whether external, internal, subjective, or objective, are dharmas.

For example, there isn't one way of being taller or smaller, older or younger, or of being here or there, north or south, "I" or "you," or of something being "good" or "bad." All of these qualities of phenomena are only designations without inherent existence in themselves. Someone who is "short" at five feet tall would appear "tall" to someone four feet tall. Thus, shortness has no independent reality in itself.

There is no birth and no cessation. There is no impurity and no purity. There is no decrease and no increase.

Birth and death also need to be analyzed in the same way we look at "I," cars, football teams, and karma. Avalokiteshvara continues the teaching by saying that the qualities of one's intrinsic nature never cease. Obscurations cannot cause the essential nature to decrease, nor can any external force cause the enlightened qualities to increase. There has never been any impurity in reality. There is nothing to be established as substantial or to be made pure through practice.

The sutra goes on to discuss the emptiness of the eighteen dhatus (consisting of sense organs, sense objects, and consciousnesses):

Therefore, Shariputra, in emptiness, there is no form, no feeling, no perception, no formation, no consciousness; no eye, no ear, no nose, no tongue, no body, no mind; no appearance, no sound, no smell, no taste, no touch, no dharmas; no eye dhatu up to no mind dhatu, no dhatu of dharmas, no mind consciousness dhatu...

We must keep remembering that this sutra is teaching from the ultimate, or absolute, point of view of the realization of a buddha. From that point of view, the "I" does not exist. This is why there is no form, no feeling, no perception, no formations, no consciousnesses, and so on.

This section of the sutra is primarily about the five senses and consciousnesses. It looks at the different divisions of sense objects and consciousnesses, as well as the interaction of those two. The skandhas, sense faculties, and sense consciousnesses are all lacking in—empty of—anything singular and lasting. If we have a hearing loss or change in visual acuity, the auditory or visual experiences will change. We will no longer have the same information coming through our five senses and consciousnesses. When we achieve higher levels of realization of the true nature, our perceived "reality" will also change.

The *Uttara-tantra Shastra* by Maitreya, a commentary on the buddha-nature, describes the experience of the buddhas (*tathagatas*) in this way:

> The authentic tathagatas are like space.
> Their six senses are the cause for experiencing external phenomena.
> They see external forms having no origination and they hear excellent speech as purity.
> They smell the pure scent of the discipline of the sugatas
> And experience the taste of the authentic Dharma of the great aryas.
> By touching samadhi they experience bliss,
> And through their self-nature they realize the way of the profound.
> If one contemplates in detail the cause of such realization,
> It brings about ultimate bliss.
> The tathagatas, like space, are free from causes and characteristics.

First, Avalokiteshvara goes through the five skandhas when he says that there is no form, feeling, perception, mental formations, or consciousness. Then he lists the dhatus, which are a classification of all knowable things and events, into eighteen elements: the six sense objects (visible forms, sounds, smells, tastes, textures, and mental objects); the six sense faculties (eye faculty, ear faculty, nose faculty, tongue faculty, body faculty, and mental faculty); and the six sense-consciousnesses, ranging from the eye-consciousness through the mental consciousness. (The sense faculties are the very subtle causes of the arising of the sense-consciousnesses.)

These eighteen dhatus are then connected with emptiness, by saying that there are no faculties (eye, ear, nose, tongue, body, mind); no objects (visible forms, sound, smell, taste, touch, dharmas); and no consciousnesses (eye-consciousness through mind consciousness).

Avalokiteshvara then goes on to connect emptiness with the twelve nidanas:

... no ignorance, no end of ignorance up to old age and death, no end of old age and death ...

The twelve nidanas are the twelve links in the evolution of a cyclic existence—a chain of cause and effect that keeps sentient beings in samsara. They start with ignorance, the first link of the chain, and go through old age and death, which is the twelfth link.

(1) Ignorance means that we are confused and do not understand reality. This is expressed through the creation or fabrication of a self, which we then believe exists as a unitary "me" that appears permanent despite the physical and mental changes that occur. The Sutra teachings of the Buddha identify this ignorance as the root cause of samsara.

Now that we believe in this "me" self, we form attachments to the things we desire and care about, such as family, friends, and desirable material things. We form aversions to those things and people we dislike or view as enemies. These feelings are what create (2) karma, because we act in accordance with our emotions and views.

Our karma causes us to take rebirth in a certain place in the six realms of samsara. For example, we were born a human being due to previous karmic imprints laid down in a subtle storehouse consciousness that lasts through our lifetimes (3). The patterns in the storehouse consciousness drew us to a human mother's womb following our death in our previous lifetime.

When consciousness unites with the fertilized egg, the three skandhas of feeling, perception, and mental formations begin to develop along with the physical form of the body and the consciousness. This is called name and form (4) and is all five skandhas. As the form (body) develops, the six senses of eye, ear, nose, tongue, body, and mind (5) also develop. We perceive and experience phenomena through these six sense organs as they make contact with objects (6). How we react to these sensations (7) can be grouped into three large categories of pleasant, unpleasant, or neutral. According to the quality of the sensation, craving develops, which leads to both desire and aversion (8). It is this desiring or avoiding along with the accompanying actions that makes karma and leaves imprints in the storehouse consciousness (9).

Throughout our lifetime, we create more causes for rebirth (10) through our actions of body, speech, and mind. Because of our karma, we will again take birth (11), age, and die (12). This endless circle of seeming endings and beginnings, birth and death, is samsara.

Nagarjuna categorized the nidanas thus: "The first, eighth, and ninth are disturbing emotions; the second and the tenth are karma; and the remaining seven are suffering." With this comment Nagarjuna demonstrates cause and effect: disturbing emotions and karma are the cause or origin of suffering. The other seven categories are the effect, which is suffering. The twelve nidanas can be summed up as two of the Buddha's Four Noble Truths: the truth of suffering and the truth of the cause of suffering.

If ignorance can be eliminated, then the chain of samsaric birth is broken. As said by Dharmakirti in the *Pramana-varttika:*

If one sees the selflessness of phenomena,
The seed of samsara is destroyed.

The Twelve Nidanas

This cycle of twelve links in the chain of cyclic existence describes three lifetimes. The first two links, ignorance and karma, are the past life. The next eight are the present life. The last two are the future life.

1. *Ignorance*: The basis of ignorance is the belief in self.
2. *Karmic formations*: Ignorance leads to kleshas, which result in actions (*karma*).
3. *Consciousness*: Actions leave karmic imprints in the consciousness.
4. *Name and form*: *Name* refers to the four skandhas of feeling, perception, mental formations, and consciousness. *Form* is the embryo in the first stage of development, into which the consciousness has been placed.
5. *Six senses*: As the form (body) develops, the six senses—the five sense organs and mind—also develop.
6. *Contact*: The six sense organs contact their objects.
7. *Sensation*: After contact occurs, pleasant, unpleasant, or neutral sensations arise.
8. *Craving*: According to the quality of the sensation, craving, and then desire or aversion, develops.
9. *Grasping*: Due to craving, objects are either desired or avoided, which leads to further imprints on the consciousness.
10. *Becoming*: Grasping actions of body, speech, and mind fully create the strong karmic imprints causing the next rebirth.
11. *Birth*: Depending on the imprints from past karma, we take birth.
12. *Aging and death*: After birth comes aging and finally death.

Finally Avalokiteshvara expresses the emptiness of the Four Noble Truths when he says:

... no suffering, no origin of suffering, no cessation of suffering, no path, no wisdom, no attainment, and no nonattainment.

Because the fundamental nature of great emptiness is without the confusion of duality, there is no suffering caused by the six kleshas: ignorance, desire, anger, pride, doubt, and wrong views.

Because of that, there is no possible origin of suffering in the great emptiness. Without an origin there can be no cessation of suffering. In that fundamental nature of great emptiness, if there is no experience of the reality of samsara, then there is no path leading to nirvana and no reason for attainment.

Just because we chant, "*no suffering, no origin of suffering, no cessation of suffering,*" it does not mean we will just stop suffering. We have to study, contemplate, and internalize these teachings so that we transform our lives. From the Mahayana point of view, suffering comes from ego-clinging. Ego-clinging arises because we believe that our five skandhas are a singular and truly existent thing we call ourselves.

The Buddha taught that there is "no form, no feeling," and so on, to show that this "me" that we believe in as a real thing is no more than a coming together and falling apart of many ever-changing elements. Remember that the Heart Sutra's teachings are from an absolute point of view. When we understand the absolute and apply it to the relative, then the fear of change and clinging to existence that cause so much suffering are removed.

In the *Ketaka Jewel*, Jamgon Mipham Rinpoche's commentary on the wisdom chapter of Shantideva's *Bodhicharyavatara*, these lines are quoted:

If one knows the emptiness of phenomena,
Then whatever is connected with karmic cause and effect

Becomes the wonder of all wonders
And the marvel of all marvels.

When we consider the skandhas, the different sense faculties, the dhatus, the nidanas, and the Four Noble Truths, the emptiness of them all is the same. From form through omniscience, throughout all of samsara and nirvana, everything is emptiness.

We have the limitless ability to analyze. Unlike our body, which is limited in what it can do, our mind has no limit to how we can think about our experiences or the abilities or qualities of mind. These mind qualities can be divided into useful and non-useful.

Useful qualities are in accord with, and lead to, a pure understanding of the way things are and how our mind really works. An example of this is the naturally occurring compassion and wisdom within us. These are qualities that, upon a direct and stable understanding of true nature, are continuous and self-arising. We need to begin to look for, notice, appreciate, and lengthen these moments of compassion and wisdom. Such qualities can be examined and strengthened through mental analysis.

Non-useful qualities are not in accord with the way things are, such as any analysis filtered through the kleshas, such as ignorance, desire, anger, pride, and jealousy. These kinds of experiences are not stable, so they are only temporary. Because they don't last, they are not real, ultimate qualities and are not in accord with our fundamental nature.

For the average person these non-useful qualities seem long-lasting because they are the ones that arise most often and we are very familiar with them. But upon reaching a direct and stable understanding of true nature, these qualities are not present, which shows that they are adventitious (coming about by chance rather than inherent) or fabricated due to confusion.

Likewise, these lifetimes we experience are something we fabricate in our minds. It's not something that is actually in accord with the way things are.

Buddhahood and Nirvana

Now Avalokiteshvara describes buddha-nature:

> Therefore, Shariputra, since the bodhisattvas have no attainment, they abide by means of prajnaparamita. Since there is no obscuration of mind, there is no fear. They transcend falsity and attain complete nirvana.

This passage says that the mind and its fundamental nature are stainless. There has never been any obscuration, so there doesn't need to be any hope in attaining buddhahood. We already possess this buddha mind; it is not something that we must attain or that is different from ourselves. Too often, we think of buddhahood as being separate from ourselves. The Buddha teaches here that there is no need to fear not attaining buddhahood, since it is something that we already have.

The fundamental root for attaining buddhahood is not our body or speech. Buddhahood is the complete manifestation of the fundamental nature of our mind. This is very important to remember when we think of attaining the fruition of buddhahood.

Gendun Chophel, a leading Tibetan thinker of the twentieth century, wrote:

> On the other side of this mist of appearances,
> One resides in reality in the sky of the meaning of dharmata.
> So-called existence is once again a fabrication.
> So-called nonexistence is once again a fabrication.
> Not tainted by all such fabrications,
> The nature of mind is the perfect Buddha.

The disturbing emotions associated with the mind's non-useful aspects continually arise because of our non-abandonment of these emotions, the appearance of physical objects that trigger the emotions, and incorrect understanding of the nature of reality. Because these kleshas are not qualities of the fundamental nature of mind, it is possible to change them.

The qualities of the fundamental nature of mind, associated with the useful point of view, are called wisdom, compassion, or bodhichitta. When this fundamental nature is fully actualized and completely understood, then this is buddhahood or complete nirvana.

Avalokiteshvara continues with the relative point of view:

All the buddhas of the three times, by means of prajnaparamita, fully awaken to unsurpassable, true, complete enlightenment.

In this sentence Avalokiteshvara is describing the path of complete awakening from a relative point of view. The relative point of view is important for a total understanding of the nature of all phenomena. Relative, ordinary phenomena are the gateways to understanding, and then experiencing, absolute truth. The views of absolute and relative are often described as the two wings that allow the bird of wisdom to fly to nirvana.

Chandrakirti, in this stanza from the *Madhyamakavatara* (Entering the Middle Way), clearly shows the relationship between the view and the two truths:

Through seeing all phenomena correctly and incorrectly,
One apprehends the two natures of phenomena.
When objects are seen correctly, it is said to be the absolute truth.
When seen incorrectly, it is said to be the relative.

A student of the Heart Sutra must always return to the understanding of inseparability. What is necessary is to change our confusion about this very point. We think we are singular and separate. We think there are parts, inside, outside, me, you, and so on.

Relative and absolute are not separate. In looking deeply and analyzing relative phenomena, we slowly come to understand inseparability. To understand inseparability is to understand the absolute. This will lead to a direct experience that is the beginning of the wisdom called prajnaparamita.

Here, when the word *prajna* is connected with *paramita*, then *paramita* literally means to go to the other shore or to the other side. This means the bodhisattva has gone from the first bhumi through the tenth bhumi. The bodhisattva has gone to the other side, to buddhahood, or from our current side, samsara, to the other side, which is nirvana.

The bhumis, the stages described in the Mahayana, refer to the process by which the fundamental nature of our mind is actualized and manifests. We haven't fully manifested the prajnaparamita as long as kleshas and false views continue to arise in our minds. As we progress on the path, and the obscuring emotions and wrong views subside, we gradually gain an understanding of the prajnaparamita. It is most important to understand that prajnaparamita is our nature. What this means is that our nature is selfless (devoid of self) and without reference point. Our true nature is nothing to focus upon, or to hold on to, since it is nonconceptual.

There is no difference in meaning between the terms *prajnaparamita* and "the fundamental nature of mind." This fundamental nature may also be called great emptiness, sugatagarbha, buddha-nature, and basic goodness.

The Prajnaparamita Mantra

Avalokiteshvara now describes the qualities of the prajnaparamita mantra:

Therefore, the great mantra of prajnaparamita, the mantra of great insight, the unsurpassed mantra, the unequalled mantra, the mantra that calms all suffering, should be known as truth, since there is no deception.

This is the mantra associated with the fundamental nature of mind. Avalokiteshvara names the five special qualities of the mantra of the prajnaparamita. The first is that it is the mantra of great insight and is connected with the wisdom of discriminating awareness. The mantra itself is this discriminating awareness.

The next quality is that it is the unsurpassed mantra, meaning it is the most sublime and supreme, because it is completely in accord with the fundamental nature. There is no other nature to look for and nothing beyond this.

The unequaled mantra means the mantra is not a product of ordinary reality and does not have ordinary characteristics. So in that sense it's not equal to, or the same as, our ordinary experience of phenomena.

It is unequal, and also it is equal, because it is identical to the undifferentiated essential nature.

When it says, "*the mantra that calms all suffering*," it means that at the point when we realize the prajnaparamita, there is no suffering, because all the kleshas and mistaken views are pacified or calmed. They no longer exist in the mind.

The prajnaparamita is our fundamental nature and so it "*should be known as truth*" and there is no falsity or mistake in it. There is no differentiation between the understanding of this mantra and prajnaparamita itself.

The sutra continues with the mantra of prajnaparamita:

The prajnaparamita mantra is said in this way:

OM GATE GATE PARAGATE PARASAMGATE BODHI SVAHA

In some texts this mantra begins with the Sanskrit word TAYATHA (or TADYATHA), which signifies that the essential nature of samsara and nirvana are one without differentiation and that all phenomena are equal in nature.

The syllable OM has a special meaning here, which is no reference point. It means that the five poisons—the five kleshas of ignorance, desire, anger, pride, and jealousy—are transformed into the five wisdom qualities of the Buddha:

> All-accommodating wisdom is transformed ignorance.
> Mirror-like wisdom is transformed anger.
> Discriminating-awareness wisdom is transformed desire.
> Wisdom of equanimity is transformed pride.
> All-accomplishing wisdom is transformed jealousy.

GATE, GATE (pronounced *gah-tay*) is translated as *gone, gone* and refers to there being no reference point or no focus. The first GATE refers to the fact that the prajnaparamita is benefiting oneself. We gain this benefit by abandoning the obscurations of the afflictive emotions, or kleshas, as well as our cognitive obscurations. In other words, due to knowledge we have gone beyond the kleshas and obscurations.

The second GATE refers to the prajnaparamita that also benefits others and is connected with attaining the state of buddhahood. Through the realization of the prajnaparamita, oneself and others benefit. One has gone from samsara completely.

PARAGATE (*pah-rah-gah-tay*) means *totally gone beyond*, so it refers to sublimely and supremely benefiting oneself. When one attains the state of buddhahood, there is nothing lacking. In that sense, PARAGATE means completely gone without need to hope for some better state for oneself.

PARASAMGATE (*pah-rah-sahm-gah-tay*) means *completely gone beyond and supremely benefiting others*. Since we have completely realized buddhahood, we can work totally for the benefit of others. At this point we've achieved the most sublime and supreme benefit, the most perfect benefit for others. This is called attaining the *rupakaya,* or the two bodies of activity for others (sambhogakaya and nirmanakaya).

What we realize are three different aspects of the Buddha called the three "bodies" or *kayas:* the dharmakaya, the sambhogakaya, and the nirmanakaya:

- The *dharmakaya* is the Buddha's realization of true nature. It is without reference point, form, or characteristics. The dharmakaya is known only by a buddha.
- The *sambhogakaya* is the energetic clarity of the dharmakaya manifesting into form. The energy of the clarity starts emanating and becomes something that can benefit beings. While bodhisattvas who are residing on the bhumis, the higher levels of wisdom, can see the sambhogakaya, ordinary sentient beings cannot.
- The *nirmanakaya* is the manifestation of the sambhogakaya that can benefit all sentient beings living in the six realms of samsara. Buddhas, bodhisattvas, and sentient beings are able to see the nirmanakaya emanated form. Shakyamuni Buddha, in his human body, is an example of a nirmanakaya manifestation.

OM GATE GATE PARAGATE PARASAMGATE is this self-liberating aspect called the three kayas, the three bodies of a buddha. The OM GATE GATE part of the mantra means the fundamental nature of emptiness, or dharmakaya. PARAGATE PARASAMGATE means the clarity of emptiness that is the sambhogakaya and nirmanakaya.

BODHI (*boh-dee*) here refers to the completely awakened and unbroken quality of compassion. The fundamental nature is self-liberating and spontaneously compassionate.

SVAHA (*swah-hah*) refers to this fact that our fundamental nature is self-liberated. Self-liberated means not liberated by something else but that it is liberation itself.

The Conclusion

Avalokiteshvara then says to Shariputra:

Thus, Shariputra, the bodhisattva mahasattva should train in the profound prajnaparamita.

Students need to train wholeheartedly and with great diligence in the practices that lead to a direct realization of the prajnaparamita. In the *Bodhicharyavatara,* Shantideva taught:

All these branches
Were taught by the Sage for the sake of the paramita of
   prajna.
Therefore those who suffer
And desire peace should give rise to prajna.

The sutra goes on:

Then the Blessed One arose from that samadhi and praised noble Avalokiteshvara, the bodhisattva mahasattva, saying, . . .

While the Buddha was in samadhi, he was surrounded by a large retinue that included Avalokiteshvara and Shariputra. It was through the Buddha's blessing that Avalokiteshvara had the same understanding and realization as the Buddha. The blessing of the Buddha also prompted Shariputra to ask Avalokiteshvara how one should practice the prajnaparamita. The exchange between Shariputra and Avalokiteshvara then followed. The Buddha was still in samadhi at that point, yet he was completely aware of what was going on. Now the Buddha speaks for the first time, saying:

"Good, good, O son of noble family; thus it is, O son of noble family, thus it is. One should practice the profound prajnaparamita just as you have taught and all the tathagatas will rejoice."

Avalokiteshvara answered Shariputra's question and the Buddha said yes, that is exactly the way it is. Excellent, excellent, that's just it! In saying this, the Buddha agreed that Avalokiteshvara was correctly understanding and explaining the prajnaparamita. As a result of that, the Buddha said, *Good, the tathagatas will rejoice.*

The sutra ends by saying:

When the Blessed One had said this, venerable Shariputra and noble Avalokiteshvara, the bodhisattva mahasattva, that whole assembly and the world with its gods, humans, asuras, and gandharvas rejoiced and praised the words of the Blessed One.

At the forefront of the retinue were Shariputra and noble Avalokiteshvara. The whole assembly included monastics, lay practitioners, and beings from other realms such as Indra, king of the devas (gods); Vemachitra, king of the asuras (jealous gods); and Zurpungapa, king of the gandharvas (celestial musicians).

All praised the words of the Blessed One and rejoiced because of Avalokiteshvara's realization, and everything he said was connected to the pure meaning. Because of this, everyone in the assembly received this wonderful transmission.

Shakyamuni Buddha generally taught in Sanskrit when giving the Mahayana teachings. Although there were many beings assembled, they all heard the teachings in their own languages. We have to remember that the Buddha was extraordinary and had been on the path for many kalpas before achieving complete enlightenment. Because of his enlightenment, his speech was extraordinary too. The disciples were able to understand things in individual ways simultaneously. It is said that the Buddha gave 84,000 different kinds of teachings, appropriate for different levels of understanding.

The teachings in the Heart Sutra are divided into three classifications: the words of consent or permission of the Buddha, the blessed words of the Buddha, and the direct words of the Buddha.

At the beginning where it says, *Thus have I heard. Once . . .* and at the end where it says, *. . . praised the words of the Blessed One,* these words are classified as the consent teachings of the Buddha, or the teachings given by permission of the Buddha, because he instructed his disciples to add them to the collection of his teachings.

The main body of the text is the words of Avalokiteshvara. It is considered a teaching of the Buddha because it was through the blessing of the Buddha that Avalokiteshvara had this realization and that Shariputra asked the question about practicing the prajnaparamita. This is called the blessed words or teaching of the Buddha.

The portion of the sutra that contains the direct words of the Buddha reads: *Good, good, O son of noble family; thus it is, O son of noble family, thus it is. One should practice the profound prajnaparamita just as you have taught and all the tathagatas will rejoice.*

Practices to Deepen Understanding of the Heart Sutra

We want to start with the five skandhas—form, feeling, perception, mental formations, and consciousness—and then move toward the state of emptiness or selflessness.

The skandhas were discussed in chapter 8, on the seal of multiplicity. Here they are being used to help us understand emptiness, so the focus is a little different. However, the understandings gained from the earlier contemplations will be helpful, since they are indirectly leading toward this conclusion.

Begin by taking refuge and arousing bodhichitta, using these lines composed by Atisha:

In the Buddha, Dharma, and Sangha
I take refuge until I attain enlightenment.
Through the merit produced by my practice of meditation
    and recitation,
May all sentient beings receive benefit and attain the state of
    enlightenment.

The following contemplations are designed to be separate practices, using one for each session. If you wish to do more than one in a session, you may move directly from one to the next without repeating the opening steps. After each session of practice, the Heart Sutra is chanted, followed by the dedication of merit.

Form

Sit in a quiet place on a cushion or chair. Relax. Feel your whole body from the crown of your head to your feet. Ask, "Who am I?" Look at your body. Consider the outside of your body. Consider the inside of your body. Take your time and go slowly and carefully. Look at your body as a whole. Then look carefully at your limbs and torso. Consider your organs and body systems. Now move to your head. Think of the parts of your eyes and then look around you. Notice the "quality" of seeing. Then move to your ears and hearing. Where is "I" in the body? This can be done using the other senses as well.

Feeling

Sit in a quiet place on a cushion or chair. Relax. Bring to mind a situation or person that you have strong feelings about, whether pleasant or unpleasant. Allow the feelings to arise along with any secondary thoughts. Then ask yourself: Where is "I" in the pleasant, unpleasant, and neutral feelings?

Perception

Before you begin this section of contemplation, find a few small objects and place them close to your meditation seat. They should be able to provide smells and sounds as well as colors, textures, and weight. For example, you might choose a piece of fruit, a watch, a colorful piece of clothing, and a pen.

Sit in a quiet place on a cushion or chair. Relax. Look around at your surroundings. Let them fill your senses. Stay with the experience for a few minutes. Then begin to pick up the objects you have selected, and use your senses to experience all the characteristics of the objects. Perceive the colors, shapes, textures, weight, and other qualities. Then ask yourself: Where is "I" in my sensory perceptions?

Mental Formations

Sit in a quiet place on a cushion or chair. Relax. Experience wherever you are, using your senses. Notice any secondary thoughts or judgments about what you are experiencing. For example, what catches your attention and why? What have you not noticed and why? Do this again and again. Then ask yourself: Where is "I" in the mental events that accompany perception?

Consciousness (Mind)

Consciousness is the stronghold of the conceptual "I."

Sit in a quiet place on a cushion or chair. Relax.

1. Allow thoughts to arise naturally for a few minutes, being aware of them but without judgment or expectation as much as possible. Then ask yourself: Where is "I" in these thoughts?

2. Observe the way the main focus of your attention moves from the various senses and their objects. For example, you may be looking at the cover of this book and then the phone rings. Your attention shifts from sight to sound. Then ask yourself: Where is "I" in the movement of the attention from the senses to the objects, and from one sense to another.

3. Beforehand, choose a few of your possessions that have special meaning to you and place them by your seat. When seated for the session, look at and hold the different possessions, and think about them. Watch the emotional content and thoughts arising in your mental consciousness. Then ask yourself: Where is "I" in these thoughts and emotions?

4. Look carefully, spending some time doing this part of the practice. Can you identify any singular, stable, solid, or truly existent characteristic (shape, color, size, weight, location, etc.) of your mental and sensory consciousnesses?

When you investigate and understand the nature of the five skandhas and the "self," the conclusion will be that there is no permanent, independent existence—our normal belief. What we assume to be true about ourselves, that we are permanent and *independent*, cannot be verified when actually investigated. At the same time, we do have an *interdependent* existence as the five skandhas, whose seeming continuity is illusory, because they are always changing.

To know that all is interdependent and illusory like a dream is a good thing. The excessive grasping and holding on to self and things as real, permanent, and "mine" make our mind and body tight and troubled. If we can understand there is nothing to hold on to in reality, our body and mind can relax. A relaxed mind is emptiness. It is joyful awareness.

Chanting

Now chant the Heart Sutra, remembering that all phenomena are empty in nature, like an illusion, not solid or permanent.

There is not one single style or tune used for chanting the Heart Sutra; each country or Buddhist tradition has its own way. At our Pema Karpo Meditation Center in Memphis, Tennessee, we chant the English text together in a group, in a monosyllabic style accompanied by rhythmic percussion. A sample of our chanting can be found on the book's website at: www.YourMindIsYourTeacher.org.

Sit silently for a while in a relaxed manner with your understanding of emptiness.

Dedicating the Merit

End by dedicating the merit to all beings.

By this merit may all attain omniscience
May it defeat the enemy, wrongdoing.
From the stormy waves of birth, old age, sickness, and death,
From the ocean of samsara, may I free all beings.

Easily memorized, the Heart Sutra can be remembered and contemplated during daily activities to promote a deeper understanding of emptiness. It is appropriate to chant and contemplate when obstacles arise, to generate merit, to subdue negative emotions, and as an aid to remembering the true nature of reality.

The Wheel of
Analytical Meditation

The Wheel of Analytical Meditation

The Complete Training in the Detailed
Examination of the Activities of Mind

Jamgon Mipham Rinpoche

The more one analyzes, the more certainty arises.
—Jamgon Mipham Rinpoche

Homage to Manjushri.

Every fault in existence
Comes about through the power of the kleshas in one's mind.
The cause of these kleshas is incorrect mental activity.
When the kleshas are relinquished, mental activity is correct.

There are three topics:
1. How to Meditate
2. Assessing One's Progress
3. The Goal

How to Meditate
Multiplicity

Wherever there is an object of particular attachment,
Envision it clearly in front of your mind
And separate it into the five skandhas.
In the beginning, fully analyze the body.

Consider the flesh, blood, bones, marrow, and fat,
The organs, limbs, and senses,
Urine, excrement, parasites, hair, nails, and so forth.
All the many unclean substances
Are composed of earth and the other elements.
Classify them into their appropriate categories.
Divide all the many things that exist,
Stage by stage up to their final particles.
Determine whether any of the parts
Give rise to attachment or not.

What is called the body is none other than
These unclean substances made up of particles.
Thus, this body is an unclean contrivance,
An assemblage like a heap of grass, a wall of stones,
A pile of manure, or a mass of bubbles.
When you consider the body, be attentive to this
    explanation.

When the continuity of your contemplation subsides,
Analyze the various aspects of each of the other skandhas:

Feeling, perception, formation, and consciousness.
When you see feeling as water bubbles,
Perception like a mirage,
Formation like a banana tree,
And consciousness like an illusion,
They will not give rise to attachment.
Continue contemplating in this way until the strength of
    your contemplation diminishes.
At that time, discontinue the detailed examination of
    multiplicity and go on to the next topic.

Impermanence

Contemplate well how all these skandhas,
Impure and without essence,
Arise and cease
Moment by moment.

All that has occurred previously in this world
Has come to an end and is no more.
The same is true for everything existing now and in the
    future.

The nature of conditioned phenomena is to cause grief.
All beings will certainly die,
And death comes suddenly, without warning.
All these appearances of cyclic existence
Are subject to circumstance and change. Contemplate this.

In summary, contemplate clearly
Each of the stages of all the many different aspects of
    impermanence
In accord with your ability.

Whenever a skandha, the object of attachment, arises,
See it as transitory,
Like lightning, water bubbles, or clouds.
Contemplate in this way
Until the strength of your contemplation diminishes.

Suffering

Each of the many skandhas,
The instant it arises,
Appears as the nature of suffering itself,
Or appears as bliss and then changes
And becomes the cause of later suffering.
The skandhas are thus the basis of suffering.
In accord with your ability,
Contemplate all the suffering that exists in samsara
And recognize that all such suffering is due to the skandhas.

Even a fraction of the mere tip of a pin
Of the defiled skandhas
Will result in suffering—such is their defect.
The skandhas, the source of suffering,
Are said to be like a filthy swamp,
A fire pit, and an island of cannibal demons.
Contemplate in this manner until the strength of your
    contemplation diminishes.

Selflessness

Afterward, ask yourself where,
In this variety of impermanent skandhas
That form the basis of suffering,
You can find anything called "I."
Through such examination, understand the notion of self to
    be empty.
See the self as a cascading waterfall, rain, or a vacant house.
Contemplate with certainty in this
Until the strength of your contemplation diminishes.
At that time, once again,
Stage by stage as before, analyze the skandhas.
Sometimes analyze without any order
Or in various ways, thus contemplating whatever is suitable.

Again and again, perform this analysis.
Sometimes contemplate the skandhas of another.
Sometimes examine your own skandhas.
Sometimes analyze all conditioned phenomena.
Wherever you find attachment, root it out.

In brief, having relinquished thoughts
That are not these four analyses,
Turn the wheel of analysis without interruption.
The more you analyze, the more profound the
    certainty.

Thus, when analyzing the variety of phenomena,
Enter with clear understanding,
And like a fire spreading through grass,
Practice continuously without break.

Before, you always engaged
In incorrect mental activity,
Perpetuating the constant flow of various thoughts.
Now, instead, remain in analysis.

When you become tired
And you are not analyzing,
If kleshas do not arise
Then simply relax in equanimity.

After a while, when refreshed from weariness,
Again perform a detailed examination as before.
At all times be mindful and attentive
To the insights gained from close analysis.

If you forget to do this practice
And the kleshas arise,
Return at once to detailed examination
As if grabbing a weapon at sight of the enemy.

Just as light illuminates darkness,
Such detailed examination,
Even practiced a little,
Harms the kleshas.
It's needless to say what significant practice would do.

Nirvana

However much one perceives
The faults of conditioned samsara,
To that extent, one will know the unsurpassable cool
    peacefulness
Of unconditioned nirvana.

Assessing One's Progress

Once one becomes trained,
One will naturally master
The five skandhas of self and others, all composite phenomena,
Their multiplicity and impermanence,
And their suffering and selflessness.
At that time, without deliberate effort,
When all appearances arise in their insubstantial multiplicity,
The kleshas will be subdued.

At that time, separated from the waves of the kleshas,
The lake of mind will be free from turbidity.
One becomes attuned to pure independence
And reaches the samadhi of shamatha.

When one sees suchness
Within the reality of one-pointed mind,
One has achieved vipashyana.
These two are the initial path for all three yanas.

The Goal

At any time, all phenomena are akin to an interdependent
 illusion
And are non-arising from the very beginning.
Thus, the emptiness of selfless phenomena is free
From distinctions of one and many and the two extremes of
 existence and nonexistence.

The space of inseparable equanimity
Is what is to be realized in the Mahayana path.
It is supremely luminous dharmadhatu.
It is also sugatagarbha.
When one realizes this, one reaches the end of samsara and
    nirvana and
Accomplishes great non-abiding nirvana.

This is supreme bliss.
This is the completely eternal great unconditioned nature.
The qualities of this great essential nature
Are the unsurpassable paramitas.

This is the meaning of the unsurpassable definitive secret
    essence.
In the space of great bliss, the co-emergent nature,
One meets self-existing wisdom itself.
Within that nature, all phenomena are complete.
Through these oral instructions of the guru,
One directly receives the pointing-out instruction, the
    manner of Great Completion.

For destroying the container of conditioned confusion,
This path of detailed examination is excellent
As the common preliminary application
For the Sutrayana and Mantrayana of the Mahayana path.

First, by the power of detailed examination,
One destroys the signs of the arising of the kleshas.
Having gained certainty in the emptiness of the skandhas,
One is free from desirous attachment to the three realms.

Then stage by stage all traces
Are fully pacified in emptiness.
Not wishing for any antidotes to eliminate the undesirable,
One is finally free from all attachment.

Through compassion free from attachment,
One is fearless in samsara whatever circumstances occur,
Flying like a bird in the space of dharmadhatu,
Attaining the state of the supreme victorious ones and their
    descendants.

In this way, in accord with the scriptures of the noble ones,
I have explained this complete training in the analysis of
    mind,
The preliminary path of shamatha and vipashyana
Which is of essential importance in the path of the three
    yanas.

To the extent one is accustomed to the detailed examination
Of this complete training in the analysis of mind,
One diminishes the kleshas;
And to the extent the kleshas are diminished,
It becomes easier to accomplish shamatha.
For example, just as fire purifies gold,
Making it malleable,
In the same way, the mind without attachment eases
    accomplishment.

Consider the merit of someone who, for one thousand diety
    years,
Meets all the needs of the Three Jewels,
Providing them whatever they require.

By comparison, if one examines the suffering,
Impermanence, emptiness, and selflessness of conditioned
    existence,
For just the time it takes to snap one's fingers,
The merit gained is immeasurably more exalted, as said in
    the sutras.

The recitation of the Four Seals of the Mahayana teachings
Is equivalent to expounding the 84,000 dharmas.
By explaining, and meditating well, on the meaning of the
    Four Seals,
One correctly meditates on the essential meaning
Of the many billions of classes of sutras.
By doing this, one obtains with little difficulty the treasury
    of profound and vast prajna
And one is quickly liberated.

In these degenerate times,
When individuals are causing excessive harm,
May the powerful amrita of the Dharma, free from
    attachment,
Enable you to reach the stage of peace.

....

Written by the all-victorious Mipham on the 18th day of the 10th
month of the Iron Rabbit year (1891).
Mangalam!

Glossary

Abhidharma (Skt., "higher Dharma"). A body of literature containing core teachings of the Buddha; an important part of the curriculum at monastic colleges. The Abhidharma describes in detail all phenomena, defining many of the topics mentioned in the sutras, and arranges them in classifications, such as the six realms of existence, the five skandhas, the eighteen dhatus, and the Four Noble Truths.

amrita (Skt.; Tib. *dutsi*). Nectar of blessings.

arhat (Skt.). A title for the Buddha and for the highest level of his noble disciples; a worthy one or pure one; a person whose mind is free of defilement and who is thus not destined for further rebirth. There are three types of arhats: hearers (*shravakas*), solitary realizers (*pratyekabuddhas*), and buddhas.

arya (Skt.). A "noble one," who has attained the direct realization of self-lessness. In the Mahayana, an advanced bodhisattva is known as an Arya Bodhisattva.

asura (Skt.). One of the classes of beings in the six realms, called jealous gods, demigods, or titans. The jealous gods are powerful, intelligent, long-lived beings whose pleasures and abundance rival those of the gods (*devas*). Their main characteristic is jealousy. They spend their time fighting and quarreling among themselves over possessions and territories. They wage war against the gods, but lose due to the superiority of the gods.

bhumi (Skt.). A stage or level of attainment. The term is used when referring to the stages a bodhisattva traverses on the path to enlightenment. There are ten bhumis, the eleventh being buddhahood.

bodhi tree. The sacred fig tree in Bodhgaya under which the Buddha attained enlightenment. A descendant of that same tree is a current site of Buddhist pilgrimage.

bodhichitta (Skt.). The wish to achieve buddhahood for the benefit of others, to help them reach ultimate happiness and enlightenment. The underlying motivation of practitioners of Mahayana Buddhism.

bodhisattva (Skt., *bodhi*, enlightenment + *sattva*, being). One who vows to attain enlightenment for the benefit of all beings and who has aroused bodhichitta, the compassionate wish to bring all beings to that state of ultimate happiness. Also, one who has attained the first through tenth stages (bhumis) of the bodhisattva path.

buddha (Skt.; Tib. *sang-gye*). The Buddha of our age is Shakyamuni Buddha. In the Tibetan term, *sang* indicates that all the emotional defilements that cause suffering no longer exist, and *gye* means increased or completely perfected qualities (wisdom, loving-kindness, omniscience, etc.).

buddhahood. Enlightenment or complete realization; the completely awakened state of a buddha.

deva (Skt.). A deva, or "god," is an inhabitant of the heavenly realms. The god realm, one of the higher three of the six realms within samsara, is the abode of blissful, long-lived beings who rarely interact with the human realm. According to Buddhism there is no "god" in the sense of a creator deity or a permanent Oversoul. *See also* asura

Dharma (Skt.; Tib. *cho*). Spiritual teachings, mainly those of Shakyamuni Buddha (the Buddha Dharma). For example, the "84,000 dharmas" are sections of the Dharma taught by Shakyamuni Buddha as antidotes to the 84,000 kleshas. *Dharma* can also refer to the realizations of dharma practitioners and to any truth. In addition, dharmas are phenomena, both external and internal, subjective and objective, anything that is interdependent, and all worldly objects with definable characteristics.

dharmadatu (Skt.). The fundamental nature of reality; the basic space in which all phenomena of samsara and nirvana arise, dwell, and cease. From the Sutra point of view, it is emptiness. Dharmadhatu is not the same as the space (*akasha*) that is the last of the five elements.

dharmakaya (Skt.). One of the three bodies or aspects (*kayas*) of a buddha; the "truth body," which refers to the Buddha's realization of the true nature of phenomena.

dhatu (Skt.). All knowable things and events are classified into eighteen elements or dhatus: six sense objects (visible forms, sounds, smells, tastes, textures, and tangible objects and mental objects); six sense faculties (eye faculty, ear faculty, nose faculty, tongue faculty, body faculty, and mental faculty); and the six sense-consciousnesses, ranging from the eye-consciousness through the mental consciousness.

disturbing emotions. *See* klesha

Dzogchen (Tib., Great Perfection or Great Completion). The highest and most profound of the wisdom teachings of Tibetan Buddhism, pointing to the nature of primordial enlightenment.

ego-clinging. Attachment and grasping that result from the belief that the five skandhas are a singular and truly existent thing that we call "I."

emptiness (Skt. *shunyata*). The absence of inherent existence in all phenomena; complete openness, without obstruction, which allows everything to occur. In the Mahayana, "great emptiness" is the fundamental buddha-nature, the emptiness of both the individual mind and all phenomena.

five paths. The paths or stages of the journey to enlightenment: the path of accumulation, the path of preparation, the path of seeing, the path of meditation, and the path of no more learning.

five skandhas. *See* skandha

Four Noble Truths. The truth of suffering, which is to be understood; the truth of the origin of suffering, which is to be abandoned; the truth of cessation of suffering, which is to be actualized; and the truth of the path, which is to be relied upon. (1) Suffering is an attribute of sentient existence. (2) Suffering is caused by desire. (3) The extinction of desire leads to the cessation of suffering. (4) The Eightfold Path— right view, right intention, right speech, right action, right livelihood, right effort, right mindfulness, and right concentration—leads to the extinction of desire and is the cause of happiness.

Four Seals. The four hallmarks of the Buddha's teaching: impermanence, multiplicity, suffering, and emptiness.

gods. *See* asura; deva

Hinayana (Skt.). One of the two general vehicles (*yanas*) or divisions of Buddhism; the other is the Mahayana. *Hinayana* is a collective term for eighteen Buddhist schools, of which only one is currently extant. *See also* shravaka; pratyekabuddha

interdependence. The Buddhist principle that all phenomena arise in interdependence with everything else, through causes and conditions. *See also* twelve nidanas.

jealous gods. *See* asura

kalpa. The period of time between a creation and a subsequent re-creation of a world or universe. The four kalpas of formation, existence, destruction, and emptiness are called a complete period or *mahakalpa* (great kalpa).

karma (Skt., "action"). The law of cause and effect. By doing virtuous actions we produce good karmic energy, and by doing nonvirtuous actions we produce bad karmic energy. These energies produce certain results (such as rebirth) according to universal laws.

klesha (Skt.). Variously translated as disturbing emotion, mental affliction, or obscuration, kleshas are thoughts or feelings that cover over the pure nature of the mind. They are the source of all the emotional or mental states that cause suffering and dissatisfaction. The six root kleshas are ignorance, desire, anger, pride, doubt, and wrong views. The five kleshas of ignorance, desire, anger, pride, and jealousy are known as the five poisons, which may be transformed into the five wisdom qualities of the Buddha.

luminous. Luminosity (sometimes referred to as clarity or luminous clarity) is the wisdom quality of the mind that illuminates or dispels confusion.

Madhyamaka (Skt.). The Middle Way, a system of analysis founded by Nagarjuna, based on the *Prajnaparamita Sutras* and considered to be the supreme presentation of the wisdom of emptiness.

mahasattva (Skt., "great being"). A bodhisattva who has attained the seventh through tenth bhumis.

Mahayana (Skt., "great vehicle"). One of the two major divisions of Buddhism, practiced in Tibet as well as China, Korea, Japan, and Vietnam.

Mangalam (Skt.). A word of blessing that traditionally appears in the last lines of Buddhist Sanskrit poetry.

mantra (Skt.; Tib. *ngak,* "mind protection"). Mantras are a combination of Sanskrit syllables recited to evoke particular qualities. Each mantra has a specific function. One of the most famous examples, used mainly to develop compassion, is the mantra of Avalokiteshvara, the Bodhisattva of Compassion: OM MANI PADME HUM.

Mantrayana (Skt.). Mantryana is another word for Vajrayana which is the main practice of Tibetan Buddhism.

mara (Skt.). A personification of confusion, wrongdoing, and temptation. In his *Jewel Ornament of Liberation* (trans. Herbert V. Guenther), Gampopa defined *mara* as "certain limiting experiences" that have "a deadening influence on life." The Buddha overcame four maras: the kleshas, the skandhas, the Lord of Death, and indolence.

merit (Skt. *punya;* Tib. *sonam*). Positive karmic imprint left on the mind or consciousness by virtuous actions. Merits are the principal cause of happiness in the present and future lives, through karmic cause and effect. We create merit by our positive actions and retain it by dedicating it for the benefit of all sentient beings.

Middle Way. *See* Madhyamaka

mindfulness. The mental faculty that holds an object in mind and does not lose it. Right mindfulness is part of the Noble Eightfold Path. Mindfulness is also the name of a form of vipashyana meditation in the Theravada tradition.

naga (Skt.; Tib. *lu*). A snake-, serpent-, or dragon-spirit. Nagas belong to both the animal realm and, as nature spirits, in the deva realm. They have the torso and head of a human and the body and tail of a snake or fish, although they can assume human form at will. They dwell in waterways, underground places, and in unseen realms, where they have their own societies and kingdoms. Nagas are often the custodians of treasures, either material treasures or texts. Legends say that Nagarjuna (c. 150–250) brought the *Prajnaparamita Sutra* from the realm of the nagas.

nidana. *See* twelve nidanas

nirmanakaya (Skt.). The emanation body, or physical form, in which an enlightened mind appears in order to benefit ordinary beings. It is one of the three bodies of a buddha.

nirvana (Skt.). Freedom from samsara; the cessation of ignorance and disturbing emotions. In the Hinayana teachings, nirvana is the liberation from the cycle of rebirth and suffering, the goal of spiritual practice. In the Mahayana, the nirvana of a buddha is beyond both samsara and the Hinayana Buddhist's nirvana. From the Mahayana point of view the nirvana of the shravakas and pratyekabuddhas is not complete because there are still very subtle cognitive obscurations that have not yet been purified.

noble one. *See* arya

obscuration. *See* two obscurations

paramita (Skt., "transcendent perfection"). Any of six virtues that the bodhisattva must perfect in order to reach buddhahood, according to the Mahayana: (1) generosity (Skt. *dana;* Tib. *jinpa*); (2) discipline or ethics (Skt. *shila;* Tib. *tsultrim*); (3) patience (Skt. *kshanti;* Tib. *sopa*); (4) diligence or joyful effort (Skt. *virya;* Tib. *tsundru*); (5) meditative concentration (Skt. *shamatha* and *vipashyana;* Tib. *shi-ne* and *lhakthong*); (6) wisdom (Skt. *prajna;* Tib. *sherab*).

parinirvana (Skt.). The final passing beyond suffering at life's end by buddhas and highly realized masters.

prajna (Skt.; Tib. *sherab,* "supreme knowledge"). Wisdom; the precise discernment of all things and events; discriminating awareness. Wisdom is the ability to directly know and experience the fundamental nature of all phenomena, which is emptiness. Prajna, the insight into emptiness, is one of the six paramitas.

prajnaparamita (Skt., "perfection of wisdom" or "knowledge gone to the other shore"). The highest wisdom. *Prajnaparamita* also refers to a group of sutras, or teachings by Shakyamuni Buddha, on the wisdom of emptiness and the path of the bodhisattva; and to the embodiment of wisdom as the Mother of the Buddhas.

pratyekabuddha (Skt., "solitary realizer"). A buddha who remains in seclusion and does not teach the Dharma to others through words. The path of the pratyekabuddhas is called the Pratyekabuddha-yana.

preta (Skt.). "Hungry ghost," one of the classes of beings in the six realms. Pretas suffer intensely from hunger and thirst. This is symbolized by their small mouths and narrow throats, which are unable to satisfy their large bellies.

pureland. A blissful realm that has come into existence due to the power and aspiration of a buddha. Every buddha, such as Shakyamuni and Amitabha, has a pureland.

Refuge Vow. A formal commitment to take refuge in the Buddha, the Dharma, and the Sangha (the Three Jewels); part of committing oneself to the Buddha Dharma.

samadhi (Skt.). The state of concentrative meditation or meditative absorption.

sambhogakaya (Skt., lit. "perfect-enjoyment body"). One of the three bodies of a buddha. The "enjoyment body" is the form in which the enlightened mind appears in order to benefit highly realized bodhisattvas. It is the radiant wisdom aspect of our original nature.

samsara (Skt.). The world of rebirth and death; the succession of rebirths until liberation is attained; the cycle of birth and death in the six realms of existence.

sangha (Skt.). The ordinary sangha is the community of monastic and lay practitioners, or the Buddhist community as a whole. The Noble Sangha are buddhas and Arya Bodhisattvas. The Sangha referred to in the Refuge Vow is the sangha of Arya Bodhisattvas. who have realized ultimate bodhichitta.

shamatha (Skt.; Tib. *shi-ne,* pronounced *shee-nay*). A form of resting meditation in which the mind is peacefully abiding and is not disturbed by thoughts or emotional states.

shravaka (Skt., "hearer"). A follower of the Hinayana whose goal is to become an arhat and achieve personal liberation. The shravakas' path is called the Shravaka-yana.

six realms. The realms of samsaric existence: the realms of the gods, (*devas*), jealous gods (*asuras*), humans, animals, hungry ghosts (pretas), and hell-beings (in the hot and cold hells).

skandha (Skt., lit. aggregate, heap, pile). The skandhas are a gathering of components that produce the illusion of a self. Sentient beings with form are composed of five skandhas, which come together at birth and separate at death. They are (1) form, which includes all things physical; (2) feeling, which is grouped into three categories according to whether they produce attraction, aversion, or indifference; (3) perception, the recognition of the features of an object (shape, color, etc.); (4) mental formations, which include both virtuous and nonvirtuous states; and (5) consciousness, including the five sense-consciousnesses (sights, sounds, smells, tastes, touch) and the sixth consciousness, mind.

storehouse consciousness (Skt. *alaya*). One of the eight consciousnesses. This storehouse serves as the repository of the seeds or imprints of habitual patterns and karmic impressions of past actions.

suchness (Skt. *tathata; dharmata*). The ultimate nature of reality; empty self-nature.

sugata (Skt., "gone to bliss"). An epithet of Shakyamuni Buddha or a buddha.

sugatagharbha (Skt.). Buddha-nature.

Sutra. Teachings of Shakyamuni Buddha; a text based on the Buddha's words.

Sutra school. *See* Sutrayana.

Sutrayana (Skt.). The path encompassing the teachings of the Hinayana and Mahayana, known as the "causal vehicle," because it establishes the cause for attaining enlightenment.

tathagata (Skt.). One who has become "thus-gone" or enlightened; an epithet of the buddhas. The term usually denotes Shakyamuni Buddha, although occasionally it is also used for any of his arhat disciples.

Three Jewels. The Buddha, the Dharma, and the Sangha. The object of refuge for Buddhists. Also called the Triple Gems.

three realms. The desire realm, the form realm, and the formless realm.

transcendent knowledge. *See* prajnaparamita

Tripitaka. The three collections, or "baskets," into which the Words of the Buddha are divided. They are the Vinaya, Sutra, and Abhidharma.

twelve nidanas (Skt.). The twelve steps, or links of interdependence, in the chain of cyclic existence that bind sentient beings to samsara. By eliminating ignorance, the chain of samsaric birth is broken. See page 191.

two obscurations. Two types of obscurations prevent complete enlightenment: passion-based obscurations, based on disturbing thoughts and emotions (kleshas); and the more subtle knowledge-based or cognitive obscurations. When both are removed completely, the great bliss of full enlightenment is revealed.

two truths. (1) Relative or conventional truth and (2) ultimate or absolute truth. The two truths are interdependent, but usually only relative truth is perceived. A practitioner who has realized emptiness perceives ultimate truth in a state of meditation and relative truth when leaving the meditative state. Buddhas alone can perceive both truths at once.

vipashyana (Skt.; Pali, *vipassana;* Tib. *lhakthong*). Investigation into the way things truly are, in order to develop the wisdom of emptiness. Vipashyana is one of the two primary forms of meditation and is called insight or mindfulness meditation in some schools. Contemplative Meditation, or analytical meditation, is a form of vipashyana.

Biographical Notes

Shakyamuni Buddha

Shakyamuni Buddha, the Buddha of our age, is regarded as the founder of Buddhism, although his teaching, known as the Dharma, is universal and belongs to all people. He was born in the sixth century B.C.E. in what is now Nepal, as the prince of the Shakya clan (thus he became known as Shakyamuni, or Sage of the Shakyas). His parents, King Shuddhodana and Queen Mahamaya, named him Siddhartha Gautama.

The handsome young prince was raised according to his Hindu caste of warriors and rulers, and grew to be an intelligent leader and skillful archer and horseman. He had great wealth and lived happily with his wife and son. He possessed all that anyone would desire for a life of luxury, pleasure, and comfort.

Throughout his youth Siddhartha had been sheltered from influences outside the palace because his father feared he might renounce the world, owing to a prophecy made when Siddhartha was an infant. On an excursion outside the palace with his attendant, Siddhartha witnessed for the first time the true condition of human beings, represented by the four sufferings: birth, old age, sickness, and death. As a result he became dissatisfied with his life and was inspired to search for knowledge. He began to look for another way of life that would lead to the end of suffering. At the age of twenty-nine, Siddhartha abandoned his life of ease to study with the wisest teachers of the time. He meditated for six years. He followed extreme asceticism by limiting food and drink while doing strenuous yogic practices. During that period he became very thin and weak.

Then Prince Siddhartha was offered, and accepted, a little milk curd with honey. His body became stronger. This led him to adopt the view of the middle way, which says that too much and too little are both extremes and should be avoided.

The prince sat down under a fig tree (now known as the Bodhi Tree) with a strong commitment, saying, "Even if my skin rots and my bones fall apart, I will not move from this place until I am enlightened." By the late evening he had tamed and completely abandoned the four hindrances to spiritual freedom: the disturbing mental and emotional states (the kleshas), the five aggregate factors of samsara (the skandhas), death, and indolence.

Early the next morning, upon completely realizing the true nature of existence, free from all confusion and obstacles, he became enlightened. At the age of thirty-five he attained supreme enlightenment and thereafter was called the Buddha, meaning the Awakened One.

The Buddha saw very clearly why beings suffer so terribly. It is because we do not understand how to see our own true nature directly and without doubt. He also saw that every sentient being has the potential to be fully awakened, to become a buddha. Great compassion arose naturally within the Buddha, the wish to awaken beings from their confusion and bring them the ultimate happiness of nirvana. Through the power of his love and compassion he taught for forty-five years, from his enlightenment until his *parinirvana*, or final passing away.

In the "three turnings of the wheel of Dharma," the Buddha gave a variety of teachings, in different places at different times, and in different ways according to the understanding of various people. In the first turning of the wheel of Dharma he taught the Four Noble Truths and three categories of teachings called the Tripitaka: the Vinaya, or monastic discipline and ethics; the Sutras, or basic practices and instructions; and the Abhidharma, which includes psychology, metaphysics, and cosmology. The teachings of the first turning came to be known as the Hinayana, or "lesser vehicle." The Hinayana emphasizes liberation from samsara as a goal of the individual.

The view of the Mahayana, the "greater vehicle," was taught in the second and third turnings of the wheel of Dharma. The Mahayana practitioner aspires to the bodhisattva ideal of universal enlightenment for all sentient beings. In the sutras of the second turning of the Wheel of Dharma, the Buddha taught about compassion and emptiness, the absence of inherent existence in all phenomena. The third turning focused on the buddha-nature.

Jamgon Mipham Rinpoche

Jamgon Mipham Rinpoche (1846–1912)—also known as Ju Mipham Jamyang Namgyal, Mipham the Great, and Lama Mipham—was one of the greatest lamas that Tibet has ever known. A brilliant scholar of the Nyingma lineage and a master of the Ri-me (Nonsectarian) movement, he was a prolific author. His *Wheel of Analytical Meditation,* the focus of the present book, is just one among a vast output of original teaching texts, commentaries, and other writings filling thirty-two Tibetan volumes. Mipham mastered a range of subjects, including medicine, poetry, logic, cosmology, astrology and divination, alchemy, painting and sculpture, and engineering. It is said that he wrote while simultaneously in continuous meditation, day and night. It is due to his work that the modern Nyingma school has Buddhist Universities and learned scholars.

Born to an aristocratic family in Do-Kham, Eastern Tibet, Mipham began to read, write, and memorize sacred texts by the age of six. At age twelve he entered a branch of the famous Shechen monastery, where he proved himself an unusually gifted student.

At the age of eighteen he went on a pilgrimage to central Tibet and visited all the holy places of Guru Rinpoche (Padmasambhava). During his journey to other holy sites, while performing devotional practices he is said to have experienced initial enlightenment. He also came to the intuitive realization of himself as an emanation of Manjushri, the Bodhisattva of Wisdom, although out of humility this was not revealed during his lifetime, except to a few intimate disciples. His name Jamgon is an epithet of Manjushri meaning "Gentle Protector."

In his travels, Mipham met his root teacher, Jamyang Khyentse. He spent much of this period receiving teachings and empowerments from him, as well as Paltrul Rinpoche and other masters.

Although Mipham Rinpoche was never formally enthroned at any monastery as an official tulku, or reincarnation of a past lama, his renown spread throughout the world, and his works have become the foundation of study not just for the Nyingma lineage of Tibetan Buddhism, but also for Kagyu practitioners and others. But Mipham's greatest achievement was not his scholarly work. Rather, it was the years he spent as a yogi alone in the wilderness. This is something intangible, which cannot be counted in terms of the books and texts for which he is remembered.

Near the end of his life he revealed to some of his close disciples how in meditation he had experienced his previous lives going backward through time and therefore knew the history of his stream of consciousness. He told his disciples, "For as long as the universe endures, I shall engage in bodhisattva activity, incarnating in various pure realms, and from thence sending emanations of myself into the world, for the sake of all sentient beings."

Acknowledgments

I am very grateful to have had the opportunity to write this book. Do you remember the Buddhist view of interdependence? Nothing comes from one cause and one condition, and this book has many causes and conditions.

I wish to thank the people who have helped with this book. From beginning to end, Candia Ludy has worked very hard. As my secretary, she is like my hands, and without hands it is hard to accomplish a book. Gerry Wiener and Christoph Klonk translated for me as I taught this material to students of Shambhala International. Additionally, Gerry assisted in the translation of texts found in the book. Larry Mermelstein and the Nalanda Translation Committee kindly gave permission to reprint their Heart Sutra translation. The transcribers of the teachings were Chuck Sullivan, Katharine Hall, and Susan Buck. Guru Gyaltsen created the artwork.

My thanks to Ivan Bercholz of Shambhala Publications for recommending the publication of this book. Especially I wish to express my deep appreciation of and thanks to Kendra Crossen Burroughs, the great editor of this book, whose many questions, comments, and skillful editing made the big difference.

Gratitude is also due to John Golebiewski, assistant editor at Shambhala Publications, as well as the other staff members and designers who contributed their skills and talents to bringing the book to completion.

About Pema Karpo Meditation Center

Pema Karpo Meditation Center was founded by Khenpo Gawang Rinpoche and is the main seat of his activities. Located on eleven acres in Memphis, Tennessee, Pema Karpo is inspired and guided by the teachings of Nyingma Tibetan Buddhism. We welcome all who are sincerely interested in meditation and the study of Dharma. Our regular sessions are offered online too for those who do not live in the area. Teachings, information, and schedules can be found at our website: www.pemakarpo.org.

At www.YourMindIsYourTeacher.org we have created a website for those who wish to work with this book's content but do not have a local teacher or center. There you can find further teachings by Khenpo Gawang Rinpoche on subjects from this book. FAQs, additional content to assist and guide your contemplations, and a lively student-driven forum are available. You are invited to become part of this online Contemplative Meditation sangha and join in the discussion with your questions, ideas, and insights.

Please come by and visit Pema Karpo if you are in our area. We are located at 3921 Frayser Raleigh Road, Memphis, TN 38128. Phone us at (901) 377-4834 or e-mail pemakarpo@pemakarpo.org.